UNCOVERING ANCIENT FOOTPRINTS

Related Titles by Michael E. Stone

Adam and Eve in the Armenian Tradition, Fifth through Seventeenth Centuries. Early Judaism and Its Literature 38. Atlanta: Society of Biblical Literature, 2013.

Armenian Apocrypha Relating to Abraham. Early Judaism and Its Literature 37. Atlanta: Society of Biblical Literature, 2012.

Armenian Apocrypha Relating to Angels and Biblical Heroes. Early Judaism and Its Literature 49. Atlanta: SBL Press, 2016.

Armenian Inscriptions from Sinai: Intermediate Report with Notes on Georgian and Nabatean Inscriptions. Sydney: Maitland, 1979.

The Armenian Inscriptions from the Sinai. Edited by Michael E. Stone. With appendixes on the Georgian and Latin inscriptions by Michel van Esbroeck and William Adler. Harvard Armenian Texts and Studies 6. Cambridge: Harvard University Press, 1982.

Rock Inscriptions and Graffiti Project: Catalogue of Inscriptions. 3 vols. Resources for Biblical Studies 28–29, 31. Atlanta: Scholars Press, 1992–1994.

A Textual Commentary on the Armenian Version of IV Ezra. Septuagint and Cognate Studies 34. Atlanta: Scholars Press, 1996.

UNCOVERING ANCIENT FOOTPRINTS

Armenian Inscriptions and the Pilgrimage Routes of the Sinai

Michael E. Stone

SBL PRESS

 PRESS

Atlanta

Copyright © 2017 by Michael E. Stone

All rights reserved. No part of this work may be reproduced or transmitted in any form or by any means, electronic or mechanical, including photocopying and recording, or by means of any information storage or retrieval system, except as may be expressly permitted by the 1976 Copyright Act or in writing from the publisher. Requests for permission should be addressed in writing to the Rights and Permissions Office, SBL Press, 825 Houston Mill Road, Atlanta, GA 30329 USA.

Library of Congress Cataloging-in-Publication Data

Names: Stone, Michael E., 1938– author.
Title: Uncovering ancient footprints : Armenian inscriptions and the pilgrimage routes of the Sinai / by Michael E. Stone.
Description: Atlanta : SBL Press, 2017. | Includes bibliographical references and index.
Identifiers: LCCN 2016056516 (print) | LCCN 2016057082 (ebook) | ISBN 9781628371734 (pbk. : alk. paper) | ISBN 9780884142164 (hardcover : alk. paper) | ISBN 9780884142157 (ebook)
Subjects: LCSH: Archaeological expeditions—Egypt—Sinai. | Inscriptions, Armenian—Egypt—Sinai. | Christian antiquities—Egypt—Sinai. | Armenians—Egypt—Sinai—History. | Sinai (Egypt)—Antiquities. | Sinai (Egypt)—Description and travel.
Classification: LCC DT56 .S76 2017 (print) | LCC DT56 (ebook) | DDC 915.31—dc23
LC record available at https://lccn.loc.gov/2016056516

Printed on acid-free paper.

Contents

Figures and Maps vii

Introduction: The Armenians 1
    Sinai Scenes 1   3

1. How It All Started 5

2. The First Expedition, 4–5 March 1979 11
    Sinai Scenes 2   14
    Sinai Scenes 3   25

3. The Second Expedition, 9–17 May 1979 29
    Sinai Scenes 4   40
    Sinai Scenes 5   43
    Sinai Scenes 6   43
    Sinai Scenes 7   49
    Sinai Scenes 8   54

4. The Third Expedition: The Central Sinai Route,
   16–18 June 1979 67
    Sinai Scenes 9   76
    Sinai Scenes 10   86

5. The Fourth Expedition: Mount Sinai, 23–25 February 1980 93

	Sinai Scenes 11	107
6.	The Fifth Expedition, 14–18 July 1980	121
	Desert Emptiness	137
	Sinai Scenes 12	148
7.	Negev Diary, 19–21 April 1990	153

Retrospective, 2016 161

Bibliography 163

Index 167

Figures and Maps

Figures

1.	Sandstone nodule, Wadi Ḥajjaj	3
2.	Aerial photo of Wadi Ḥajjaj and 'Ein Ḥudra	15
3.	The descent to 'Ein Ḥudra from the head of Wadi Abu Ghad'ayat	15
4.	Wadi Ḥajjaj, Rock III	19
5.	At work in Wadi Ḥajjaj	20
6.	Superimposed inscriptions and crosses, Rock III at Wadi Ḥajjaj	24
7.	Greek map of Saint Catherine's Monastery and region	33
8.	The mouth of Wadi Leja: Jebel Safsafa on the left, Mount Catherine on the right, the administration buildings in the foreground	36
9.	Tom and Uzi examine the overhanging rock, Wadi Maghara; bedouin mother and child in background	39
10.	Rock drawings and Nabatean inscription	41
11.	The sand dune at Wadi Rum	56
12.	At 'Ein Aḥdar	70
13.	The Tih and Naqb Rakna	73
14.	An acacia in the Sinai	81
15.	Charles Doughty from the frontispiece of the 1926 edition of *Arabia Deserta*	88
16.	Byzantine paving in Wadi Leja	90
17.	Bill Adler at Saint Catherine's new hostel, 1980	97
18.	Our room in the hostel at Saint Catherine's	101
19.	The author mounting the defile on Abbas Pasha's path	103
20.	Bill Adler working on the peak of Jebel Musa	106
21.	Goats and inscriptions on Rock III, Wadi Ḥajjaj	126
22.	'Ein Ḥudra	128

23. Bedouin men near ʿEin Ḥudra   129
24. Ad hoc flint tools, Wadi Zalaqa   136
25. Uzi and the jeep at Jebel Abu Ghad'ayat   149
26. Wadi Abu Ghad'ayat   150
27. Wadi Ḥajjaj, Rock XIII with Nabatean and rock drawings   151

Maps

1. The routes traveled   10
2. From Nweiba to Wadi Ḥajjaj   13
3. Wadi Maghara to Saint Catherine's Monastery   38
4. From Naqb Rakne to Wadi Abu Natash   71
5. Eilat to Wadi Zarniyeh   120

Introduction: The Armenians

I must preface this record with some words of explanation. I am a professor of Armenian studies. That alone makes me a rare bird. Having grown up in Australia in the 1940s and 1950s, I have no conscious memory of even hearing of Armenians before I went to university. There, studying classics and Semitic studies, I read of Armenian translations of ancient Jewish works. Indeed, until I was a doctoral student, I had only the sketchiest knowledge about anything Armenian.

The Armenian homeland is in the Caucasus, the rocky and mountainous area north of present-day Iraq, its heartland lying between the Black Sea and the Caspian. According to tradition, King Tiridates III (287–330 CE) converted to Christianity in 301, and so it was that Armenia became the first Christian nation, three decades before the more celebrated conversion of Emperor Constantine the Great.

The Armenians spread from their homeland in the course of the first millennium and developed a diaspora that still sprawls over much of the Middle East and beyond. The earliest Christian pilgrims to the Holy Land included Armenians; indeed, the very first pilgrim whose name we know was an Armenian, Eutaktos from Anatolia. He came in the 360s, the days of Constantine's son, Constantius. From this auspicious beginning, Armenian pilgrims streamed to the holy places through the centuries. It was pilgrims who wrote the ancient inscriptions that were the object of my search.

Inscriptions are the only dated Armenian writing before the ninth century, and the oldest inscription known before our work in Sinai was from the end of the fifth century, roughly a century after the invention of the Armenian alphabet. Our discoveries changed this situation, and the story I will tell is of how that happened.

Through inscriptions, I had become fascinated with the history of the Armenians in the Holy Land, natural enough, I suppose, for a scholar of Armenian living in Jerusalem. In the unique chapter of my life recounted here, three of my interests united: Armenian writing, inscriptions, and Armenian Holy Land pilgrimage.

I base this book on my journals recording five expeditions in search of Armenian inscriptions on the rocks of the Sinai Desert. The Armenian pilgrims, bent on reaching Mount Sinai, remain shadowy figures, but their graffiti incised on the desert's rocks are clearly identifiable. We traced them across the striking landscape of the Sinai, following—and sometimes discovering—the routes they traveled to the sacred mount. The impact of the desert itself, its majesty and its starkness, was profound. I am also a poet, and in poems I wrote about the feelings it evoked. These poems are part of the record, and I have introduced some into this account.

I have been a long time in turning my personal diary into this book. In recent years, I have had help and encouragement from my friend Lorenzo DiTommaso. Uzi Avner also always graciously answered my queries. The manuscript was edited in Jerusalem by Yael Moise. I am indebted to Roie Frieden, a wonderful photographer whose work is to be seen in figures 1, 2, 7, and 24. Cartographer Mitia Frumin produced the fine maps. My thanks are extended to SBL Press, particularly to Nicole Tilford and Bob Buller. The final editing was accomplished in an exemplary fashion. All helped me to avoid repetitions and tautologies.

My five visits to the desert, between March 1979 and July 1980, were unlike anything I have ever experienced. As time passes, the details fade from memory; only my journals, written up directly after each trip, preserve them.

I wrote the journals in the present tense, as events unfolded and in a changing political situation. Israel controlled the Sinai until 1982, and my visits took place before the Israeli withdrawal and the Sinai's reversion to Egyptian sovereignty. I retain the immediate narrative tense and the context of Israeli military government, for that was my experience. As I write these words in 2016, all that is only a memory. Today the Sinai is a scene of struggles between Islamic terrorists and the Egyptian army. How fortunate that I traveled there when I did.

Michael E. Stone
Jerusalem, January 2016

SINAI SCENES 1

Wilderness and not desert.
sandstone, cliffs, oases, wells.
not Sahara's sweeping sandy dunes.

A water-hole with palm trees
deep in a crevasse,
tall fronds scarce reach ground level.

Virginal sandy flats,
perhaps never trodden,
for footprints last millennia,
and worn paths seven thousand years.

MES

Fig. 1. Sandstone nodule, Wadi Ḥajjaj. These sandstone balls are often found on ledges of rock, having been rounded by the winds over centuries.

1
How It All Started

I became involved in this story by chance, but what a fortuitous chance! In the spring of 1978 I was invited to give a guest lecture at Andrews University in Berrien Springs, Michigan. After the lecture, I met a professor who had spent the previous year at the Albright Institute for Archaeology in Jerusalem. While regaling me with stories of his visit, he mentioned seeing a site in the Sinai covered with inscriptions, including some in Armenian. This was the first time I heard of the Armenian inscriptions in Wadi Ḥajjaj (Ḥaggag), the Valley of the Pilgrims, in western Sinai.[1] Perhaps I should have known about them already, for later I discovered that a year earlier Hebrew University Professor Abraham Negev had published a book on the Greek and Nabatean inscriptions at this site and had mentioned Armenian. But I didn't; inscriptions in the desert did not interest me then.

I could only get further information in the autumn of that year, when I returned to Jerusalem. I had requested a friend at the University's Institute of Archaeology to ask Professor Negev for photographs of the Armenian inscriptions, and he had graciously sent photographs to my office, where I found them. Impatiently, I extracted them first from the heap of mail awaiting me on my return from the United States. I saw immediately that some of the inscriptions were indeed in Armenian, and they seemed to be old. I was thunderstruck, even more by their antiquity than by their existence. I was impelled to see them. At once I bought Negev's book, which I had been unable to see while away. In it he had noted the existence of five Armenian inscriptions in the Wadi Ḥajjaj area.

How does one know when inscriptions are old? There are several approaches to answering this question. Sometimes an inscription (or a

---

1. *Wadi* means "valley" and is a common element of place names in the Sinai. Some of the wadis formed major travel routes in the desert. *Ḥajjaj* derives from the Arabic word for "pilgrimage."

manuscript) actually contains a date. When it does not, study of the material on which the manuscript was written may help; obviously, for rock inscriptions this method is not relevant. Another possible dating criterion is always available: the actual writing, the shape and form of the letters. Styles of writing change over the centuries; try reading a handwritten letter from the nineteenth century! If we know when specific changes occurred, they can help us date the script.

The Armenians began writing at the start of the fifth century CE. The oldest dated manuscript that survives is a copy of the four gospels, now in Venice, written in 862 CE—centuries after the invention of Armenian writing. My interest in writing next led me to inscriptions; they, being mostly on stone, last longer than paper, papyrus, or parchment manuscripts, and so are earlier evidence for writing than manuscripts.

Clearly, pilgrims had left these inscriptions. Armenian pilgrims were attracted to the Holy Land from the fourth century CE, if not earlier. Their presence attested the same piety and devotion that brought large numbers of Christian pilgrims from many lands to the holy places. The sanctity of the holy places often led pilgrims to settle in them, so some of the Armenian pilgrims stayed. Indeed, today there is still a sizeable Armenian community in Jerusalem whose origins are very ancient. The community maintains major cultural institutions in the city: a seminary for training priests, a high school and primary school, an excellent library, a printing press, and a collection of manuscripts.

Eutaktos is the first Armenian pilgrim whose name is known. He was an Armenian from Satala, near Melitene in Armenia Minor (in today's Turkey), who visited the Holy Land about 360 CE. Many others came in Eutaktos's footsteps, eager to tread the soil of the biblical holy places, but only few undertook the arduous trip across the desert to Mount Sinai. Eutaktos did not go there, though he did visit Egypt. One of the earliest pilgrims to make the journey to Mount Sinai was the nun Egeria, who wrote a record of her experiences for her sister nuns to read at home in Galicia in Northern Spain (about 384). In the fifteenth century, the vivacious and irrepressible German monk Felix Fabri of Ulm journeyed south from Jerusalem across the desert to the Sinai. He tells the story in his lively pilgrim book. Although nearly two hundred pilgrims had come to the Holy Land that year, only about twenty of them, the most adventurous, continued on to Mount Sinai after visiting the biblical sites in the Holy Land. Those pilgrims were the chief actors in the events we recovered, witnessed by their graffiti.

Knowledge of the history of the Armenians in the Land of Israel before the Crusader period is sparse, even more so of Armenian pilgrimages to Mount Sinai. Only one report has survived, attributed to a mid-seventh-century Greek monk called Anastasius of Sinai.

> It is the custom, he says, of the Armenians to come regularly to the holy Mount Sinai. In any case, twenty years ago, a large group of them arrived, about six hundred souls. They set out for the holy peak and when they reached the outer holy rock where Moses received the Law, a vision of God and fearful wonders took place in the holy spot to them, just as of old at the Giving of the Law. The whole of the holy peak and that group of people seemed to be covered by fire. The amazing thing was that none saw himself affected or flaming, but each saw the other as a fire. That group of people was astounded and prayed to God for mercy for about an hour. Then the fire departed from them and not a single hair of theirs was hurt, nor a garment, but their staves alone like wax in the vision, then flamed up. They continued to have the sign of burning, charred as from fire on their tops, giving witness through this appearance of theirs also in their land, as the rumour of this got about, that this day again the Lord has been seen in fire on the holy Mount Sinai.[2]

Pilgrims generally traveled on donkeys with Arab guides and approached Mount Sinai either from the west or the east. Imagine six hundred pilgrims riding donkeys, with their mounted bedouin guides, as well as additional beasts carrying baggage, food, and water! Anastasius gives no indication of the direction from which these pilgrims came or any other detail, except perhaps in that last phrase, where he refers to the Armenians' burnt staves giving witness "in their land." Does this mean that they came from Armenia? This would be likely on other grounds, for early pilgrims came from Armenia to other sites in the Holy Land.

The Armenian graffiti-writing pilgrims usually just recorded a name, sometimes with a cross. Occasionally they added a few more details, such as "I saw Jerusalem" or "I went around Sinai." One pessimistic pilgrim wrote on the peak of Mount Sinai, "Lord, have mercy on my camel and my guide." Clearly this traveler rejoiced at the climax of his journey and now was concerned about the road home.

---

2. François Nau, "Le texte grec des récits du moine Anastase sur les saints pères du Sinaï," *Oriens Christianus* 2 (1902): 81–82.

On their way to and from Mount Sinai, pilgrims had camped overnight at Wadi Ḥajjaj and had written their names on the rocks there. Pilgrimage transcended national boundaries. From Professor Negev's reports and from the photographs he had sent me, I learned that among the pilgrims were both Armenians and Georgians; Negev had not distinguished the two rather similar scripts. There is also evidence for close contact between Armenians and Greeks. Some Greek words occur in the Sinai inscriptions, and mosaic floors with Armenian inscriptions occur in Jerusalem monasteries that also housed Greeks, such as the Bird and Eustathius mosaics.[3] A unique Egyptian papyrus of the seventh–eighth centuries contains a Greek–Armenian phrasebook in Armenian script listing expressions a traveler might need and their translations. This shows that Armenians were mixing with Greek speakers, perhaps for purposes of trade as well as for pilgrimage.

Because the oldest dated Armenian manuscripts are from the ninth century CE, the most ancient dated sources for Armenian writing must be inscriptions chiseled onto stone. In 1978 fewer than twenty Armenian inscriptions from the fifth to the eighth centuries were known worldwide, so I became extremely excited when I saw Negev's photographs. The possibility of finding more old Armenian inscriptions, perhaps from the sixth or seventh centuries, was thrilling. They would teach us about pilgrim traffic and the history of the Armenians in the Holy Land. They might also contribute to the history of Armenian writing, religion, and culture. More than anything, the very surprise of there being such inscriptions in the Sinai set me back on my heels. I was entranced.

At once I started planning to go to Wadi Ḥajjaj to examine the inscriptions myself. I faced two chief difficulties. The first was that I had no experience of any sort of fieldwork. Archaeologists and geologists, botanists, and zoologists are experienced in the field, but at that time my idea of fieldwork was a drive across Jerusalem to the Armenian monastery. How was I to get to Wadi Ḥajjaj? How could I organize my visit? How should I act in the desert? These matters were great mysteries to me. My second problem was that I had to find financial support for the expedition.

To tackle the first problem, I decided to contact Avner Goren, an archaeologist who also was Staff Officer in charge of archaeology and

---

3. See Michael E. Stone, "The Greek Background of Some Sinai Armenian Pilgrims and Some Other Observations," in *Medieval Armenian Culture*, ed. Michael E. Stone and T. J. Samuelian, University of Pennsylvania Armenian Texts and Studies 6 (Chico, CA: Scholars Press, 1984), 194–202.

antiquities in the Sinai Peninsula. (Under the Israeli Military Government that controlled the Sinai from 1967 to 1982, the officers in charge of civilian activities were called Staff Officers.) It proved difficult to contact him directly, but I managed to contact his assistant, Benny Sass. Benny heard me out and said that, since the approach to Wadi Ḥajjaj was simple from Eilat, and since it was within 50 kilometers of Nweiba, a tourist center on the coast of the Gulf of Eilat, I should make my own way there. He also mentioned a single Armenian inscription he had seen at a site in the western Sinai called Wadi Maghara. That incidental remark hinted at future developments. I grew ever more excited: Armenians not just in Wadi Ḥajjaj but in western Sinai, too!

As for the problem of funding, I soon learned that the Israel Academy of Sciences and the Tarzian Chair of Armenian History and Culture at the University of Pennsylvania would support me. I had the money for the expedition. I also managed to solve the logistic problem. After a dozen calls to Eilat, someone finally referred me to Uzi Avner. Uzi is a desert archaeologist who worked, and indeed still works, in the southern Negev and Aravah area north of Eilat, and he lives in Eilat. A lover of the desert, I was told, he might join me for the trip to Wadi Ḥajjaj. I telephoned Uzi in Eilat and at once received his enthusiastic assent. Looking back now, I believe our expeditions would have been almost impossible without him. He is a fine archaeologist and extraordinarily well versed in a multitude of aspects of desert lore. His joining my expedition was the best thing that could have happened. We remain friends to this day.

Uzi's logistic skills were outstanding. It was he who made the arrangements with the jeep rental agency in Eilat; he planned our supplies, and he also drove the jeep on this trip. The other member of the expedition was Tom Samuelian. Tom, a graduate student at the University of Pennsylvania, was spending six months in Jerusalem studying with me and doing some research and studies in the Armenian monastery. He was excited about coming to the Sinai, and I was glad to have him along. It was invaluable to have another person with me who could read and record the inscriptions and with whom I could discuss the problems of their decipherment and interpretation. Indeed, Tom developed great expertise in finding inscriptions, and he actually first sighted quite a number of them, while I myself was busy with photography. I had never photographed inscriptions before, but I was experienced in photography of manuscripts. At any rate, there was no money for a photographer, so I did the job and hoped for the best.

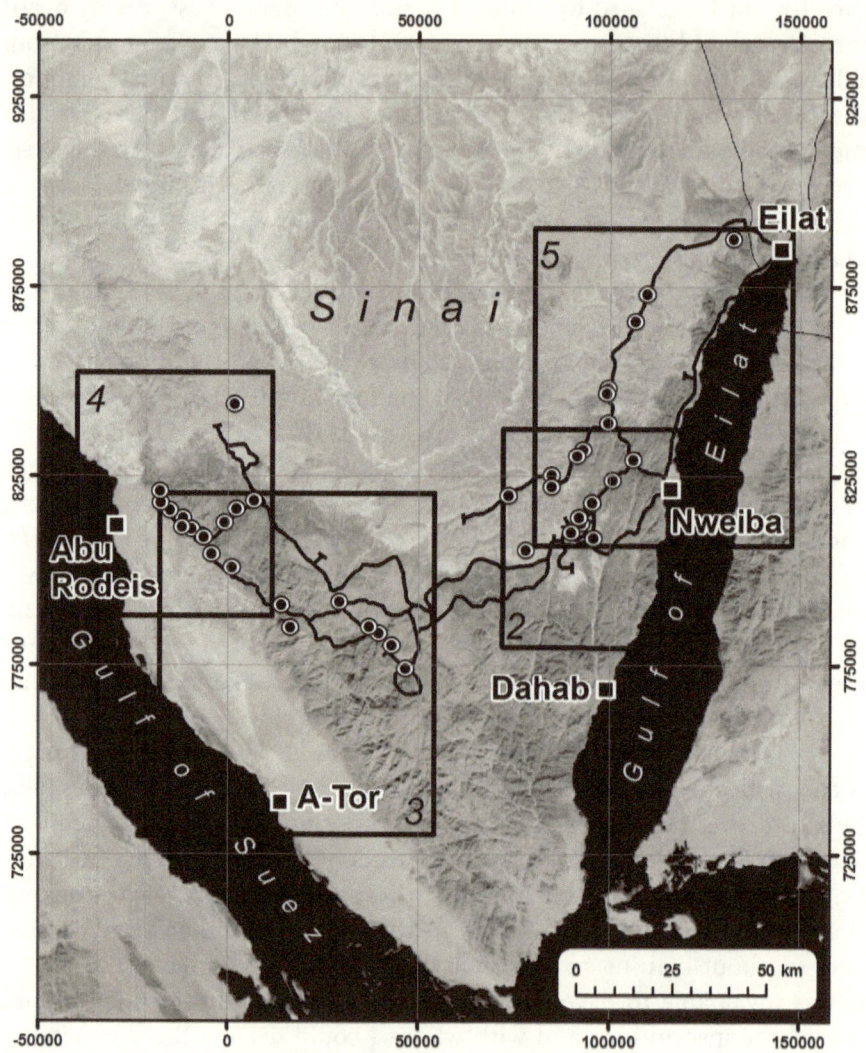

Map 1. The routes traveled

2
THE FIRST EXPEDITION
4–5 MARCH 1979

Sunday, 4 March 1979

Eilat is at the southernmost tip of the triangle of desert called the Negev ("south" in Biblical Hebrew). It stands at the northernmost point of the Gulf of Eilat, the eastern branch of the Red Sea, a twin sister of the Jordanian city of Akaba. In Roman and Byzantine times it was called Aila and was an important road station. Tom and I planned to fly from Jerusalem to Eilat, meet up with Uzi, drive to Wadi Ḥajjaj, sleep the night in Nweiba, work in Wadi Ḥajjaj the next morning, and return to Eilat in time to catch the afternoon plane for Jerusalem. I discovered later that this was a very easy trip, but even this two-day jaunt, with an overnight at the guesthouse at Nweiba, required preparations. Photographic equipment, notebooks, measuring instruments, and the like had to be readied. I did not want to discover, out in the Sinai Desert, that I needed something that was beyond reach back in Jerusalem (such as a battery for the camera!). So I erred on the side of caution and took a great deal of gear, which did not matter much on this occasion, since all our travel was by vehicle. I always aspire to travel lightly, frequently without success.

We left home for the airport in the cool early morning of 4 March. The flights south nowadays all go from Ben Gurion airport near Tel-Aviv, but at that time there were scheduled inland flights from Kalandia airport, north of Jerusalem. En route, the cab picked up Tom, and we took the 8:00 AM plane to Eilat. The flight down took under an hour.

Uzi met us at Eilat airport, and at once we went to pick up the rented vehicle, an almost brand new jeep. Although Uzi had prepared most of the gear we would need, we still had to go to the store to pick up some important supplies: sweetened cordial that we added to our drinking water and apples. Uzi had readied large lumps of ice in his freezer the previous day. He put them into the insulated water jugs; they lasted both days of the trip. To this iced water we added raspberry cordial, and we made sure that we drank continually during the day. Raspberry cordial is a cheap, sugary syrup often served in Israel when resources are limited. The danger of dehydration is quite real because in the desert the body loses moisture even though one does not always feel it. The raspberry made the water more palatable so we could drink large amounts. We bought a great many of the other item, the apples, and put them in the jeep behind the driver's seat in a bucket so we could eat them throughout the day. The apples were refreshing and filling and, in retrospect, much easier to eat with heat-chapped lips than oranges or other fruit that we took on later journeys (when apples were not in season). We did not eat a midday meal in the desert, so this was our practice on all of our trips. We found it a useful one, and I, for one, did not feel hungry, although we breakfasted early in the mornings.

We drove south from Eilat along the road that runs from Eilat to Ofira and Sharm el-Sheikh at the southern tip of the Sinai Peninsula. This road has been paved since the Israeli occupation of the Sinai in the 1967 war, and the route is scenic and impressive. It simplifies travel, but the route was not used in antiquity because the mountains come down to the sea at several places, and the supplies of water were meager and the terrain difficult.[1] As we drove south, we had the mountains of the Sinai on the right and the sea on the left. A coral reef runs parallel to the coast, and the sandy beaches all along this gulf offer wonderful swimming and snorkeling.

The two best-known sights on this road are the Coral Island (a misnomer, since it is not a coral island) and the Fjord. The Coral Island (its Arabic name is Jezirat Fara'un, "Pharaoh's Island") is off the coast but clearly visible from the road. On it is a fort, which is usually held to be a Crusader foundation with Mamluk architectural additions. However, Uzi told me that the most recent opinion is that the whole castle is post-Crusader. In any case, this small island, almost completely encircled at the top by the castle's stone walls, is a romantic sight. Somber, it stands out in striking silhouette against the intense blue of the Gulf of Eilat. Somewhat further down the coast is the Fjord. Steep mountains form the banks of an

---

1. Avner Goren, quoted in Philip Mayerson, "The Pilgrim Routes to Mount Sinai and the Armenians," *Israel Exploration Journal* 32 (1982): 44–57.

2. THE FIRST EXPEDITION, 4–5 MARCH 1979

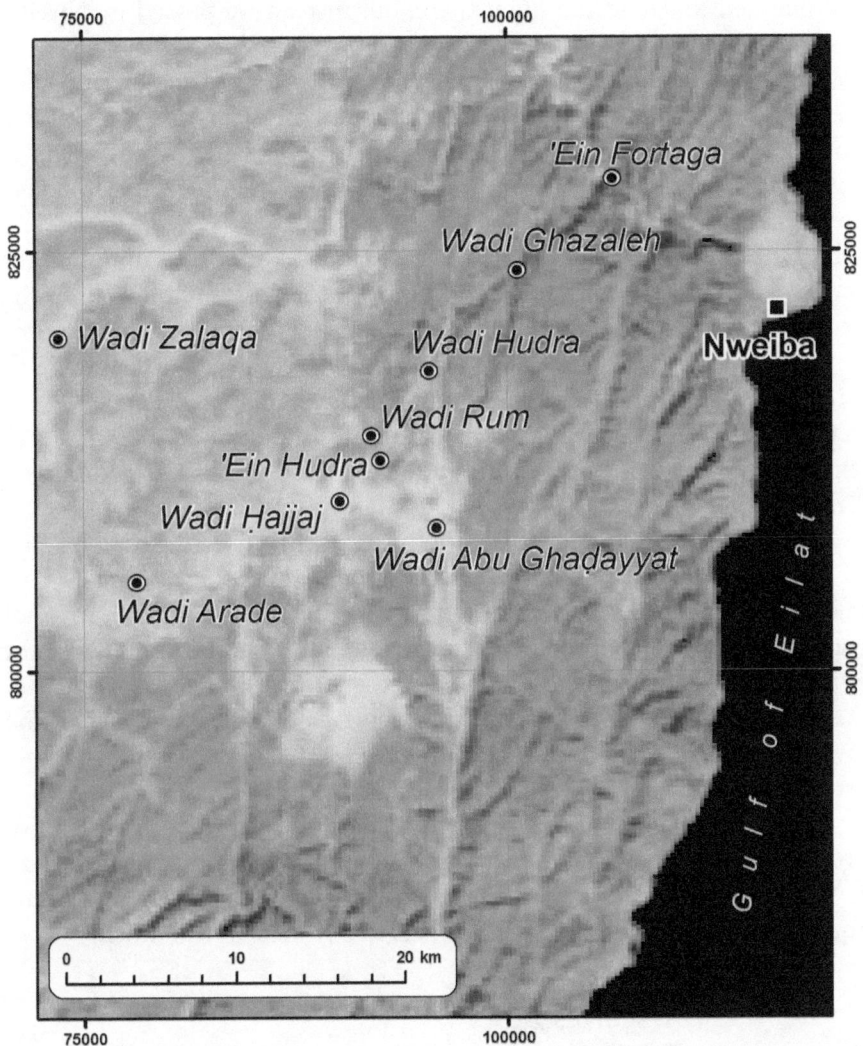

Map 2. From Nweiba to Wadi Ḥajjaj

inlet—lovely enough but miniature in comparison with the Scandinavian fjords after which it was named.

Nweiba is a vacation village on a promontory about 78 kilometers south of Eilat. Prior to that development, it was a bedouin village. A fine beach is served by a guesthouse that offers comfortable conditions. We had planned to spend the night there, but instead we passed by Nweiba without stopping.

The petrol station at Nweiba warns that it is the last one for 200 kilometers (going south, of course). This reminded me of a sign I saw at Ayers Rock in Central Australia, which showed a dripping tap crossed by a diagonal line inscribed "250"; there was no water source for 250 kilometers down that road!

Past Nweiba the road began a long, gradual climb that continued for several kilometers. We were ascending from the costal sea level into the beginnings of the mountainous massif that is the central feature of southern Sinai. Our goal, Wadi Ḥajjaj, is well above sea level, and Saint Catherine's Monastery and the area around it are even higher. The tallest peak in the Sinai is Jebel Katerina, Saint Catherine's mountain (2,629 m, 8,625 ft), adjacent to Jebel Musa, or Mount Sinai, literally "Moses's Mountain," (2,285 m, 7,496 ft).

From Nweiba to the turnoff from the coast road onto the road leading to Wadi Ḥajjaj is yet another 32 km, and then we drove 12.5 kilometers inland, altogether 122.5 kilometers (just over 76 miles) from Eilat to Wadi Ḥajjaj. The Wadi Ḥajjaj road was not paved, but it had been prepared for either tar or gravel surfacing. Much of the surface was loose stone, but the road was passable even for two-wheel-drive vehicles that are not too low slung. At the turnoff, the bedouin have erected a rough structure that serves as a kiosk.

The road takes one away from the coast and into the Sinai Desert. From a vantage point by the way, one see sandy desert on both sides, and several sites showed the scars on the sandy surface caused by road-making equipment. How vulnerable the desert is to any mechanical touch!

SINAI SCENES 2

Rain's softness never washes,
erases human tracks.
A mark made on the desert's face
remains until a blind fool
drives over it in a jeep,
crushes it under tank-tracks,
or covers it with tar.

MES

---

2. THE FIRST EXPEDITION, 4–5 MARCH 1979

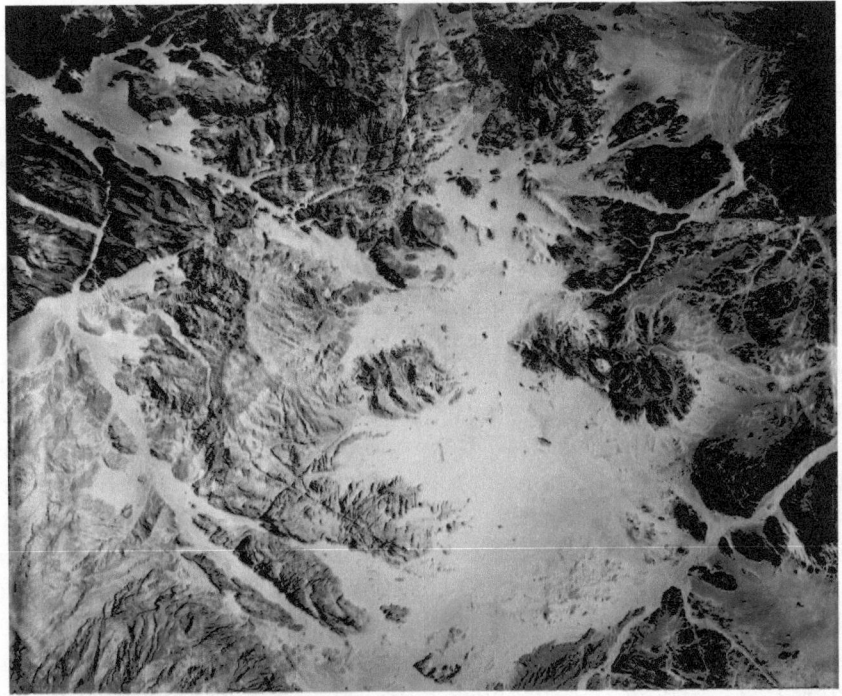

Fig. 2. Aerial photo of Wadi Ḥajjaj and ʿEin Ḥudra

Fig. 3. The descent to ʿEin Ḥudra from the head of Wadi Abu Ghadʾayat

Overall, I saw that the Israeli rule of the Sinai had been kind to the desert; there had been quite a lot of development without major scarring. I have not been back since 1982, so I cannot say how it has fared since Israel's withdrawal. Neil Folberg, a photographer and lover of the Sinai, returned after 1982. He commented in 1987, "the Egyptians have paved roads that the Israelis had left unpaved, and have built new roads that Israel had never considered building. They have built a Holiday Village at Santa Katerina, a large mosque, and they are now working on a massive concrete structure that will be, I suppose, an administrative headquarters."[2] What is absolutely clear is that the desert is terribly vulnerable, and every mark, every track made will be visible for centuries—if not millennia—unless the sand covers it! The preservation of the desert virginal is a heavy responsibility.

At that moment, though, I was excited to arrive at Wadi Ḥajjaj. The first thing I saw was a rough hut to the north of the road. This is another of the kiosks that enterprising bedouin have erected at various points throughout the Sinai. There they sell soft drinks to the passing tourists—to my surprise, there is considerable tourist traffic. There are tours not only in air-conditioned buses but also in large desert vehicles.

Wadi Ḥajjaj is a fairly wide, flat sandy area dotted with large sandstone rocks (see fig. 2). The bigger ones, such as Rocks I and III (as we called them, following Abraham Negev's numeration), were at least as big as apartment buildings. The bedouin call this sort of rock a *hadbe*. Sandstone cliffs surround the valley to the east, north, and part of the way to the west, and the road cuts across it running roughly east and west. We first drove off the road across the sand to the northernmost point of the Wadi Ḥajjaj area. There, through a pass that had been improved in recent times, we could look down on 'Ein Ḥudra below us.

'Ein Ḥudra is a green oasis with a spring at its heart a few kilometers distant from Wadi Ḥajjaj. Before the pass was opened, access to the 'Ein ("spring") was by a roundabout route that requires some time to navigate. Arthur Penrhyn Stanley, the nineteenth-century British explorer, like some others, identifies 'Ein Ḥudra with biblical Hazeroth, one of the stops of the Israelites on their desert wanderings (Num 11:35); one must admit that the names are quite similar.[3] Certainly 'Ein Ḥudra was an important

---

2. Neil Folberg, *In a Desert Land: Photographs of Israel, Egypt, and Jordan* (New York: Abbeville, 1998), 47.

3. The identification was suggested earlier by John Lewis Burckhardt, *Travels in Syria and the Holy Land* (London: Murray, 1822), 495. For a long discussion of this

stop for travelers, but its identity with biblical Hazeroth is far from certain and was probably first suggested only in the nineteenth century (fig. 3).

As we stood there viewing the site, an Egyptian vulture circled in the air above; there may have been a carcass of some sort at the spring. By now it was the middle of the day and hot. We had been drinking our raspberry cordial and eating apples, but our throats were parched and our hair white from the dust that is pervasive in these parts. Vehicles raise clouds of it, and it penetrates everywhere. Dust got into all the photographic equipment, so in the evening I had to strip down the camera and clean it meticulously with a fine brush. After the first day's experience of white hair, I kept my hat on at all times while we were moving about.

We decided to work our way systematically through Wadi Ḥajjaj starting from the northern end, where the pass to ʻEin Ḥudra is situated. Abraham Negev had recorded seven sandstone extrusions with inscriptions. Almost immediately we came upon a rock that he had not recorded, which we called Rock VIII. It is about 300 meters north of the huge Rock III. On Rock VIII we noted Arabic inscriptions, some in Greek, and some rock drawings.

Over and again Arabic inscriptions will be mentioned in this chronicle, as well as inscriptions in Nabatean and rock drawings. Most of the Arabic and Nabatean inscriptions were not connected with Christian pilgrim travel to Jebel Musa, although there are some Arabic Christian inscriptions at various sites. Certain Arabic inscriptions are quite old, while others were written in the present age. The Nabatean inscriptions, however, are all old. The Nabateans were an Arab people who lived in the desert areas in Jordan, the northern Hejjaz, the Negev, and the Sinai. Their most famous monument is the red rock city of Petra in Jordan.

The story of Nabatean writing is interesting. The great Persian Empire established by Cyrus and Darius in the fifth century BCE used Aramaic, a Semitic language close to Hebrew, as its lingua franca. The style of Aramaic writing used by the royal bureaucracy became widespread through the empire. The Nabatean script developed from it as well, as did the square Hebrew script, which is still in use. Thus, although the Nabateans were Arabs, their writing and inscriptions were in Aramaic. The present

---

identification, see Arthur Penrhyn Stanley, *Sinai and Palestine in Connection with Their History* (London: Murray, 1856), 81–83.

Arabic script developed from Nabatean and is used to write the Arabic language, which is also related to Hebrew and Aramaic.

Many mysteries remain about the Nabateans of the Sinai, but it is clear that Nabatean tribes actually lived there and did not just transit the desert. A major Nabatean center in the peninsula was at the great oasis of Feiran, in southwestern Sinai, which we visited later. In addition, they left inscriptions along the length of the major routes of travel in the Sinai, as well as in sacred places and other particular spots. These inscriptions were frequently written in large letters and are often high up on the rocks and cliffs; many of their sanctuaries were located on high mountain peaks. Most of the inscriptions simply record a man's and his father's names. Occasionally they add other elements, such as titles or wishes, as in "May X son of Y be remembered" or "May X son of Y be blessed." There are also formulas of blessing, designations of various occupations and official positions, and, occasionally, dates. The study of the names and the families and where they occur might tell us about tribal groupings and areas of control, as well as indicating the routes they traversed. Much research is yet needed to recover their history in detail, but they left traces all over the peninsula.

The Nabateans were also responsible for many of the rock drawings we saw in the Sinai. These depict various natural and human subjects, chiefly animals; camels and ibex star, but occasionally there were also canines, ostriches, and other creatures. There are scenes of hunting and of war, as well as fertility drawings of various types, and footprints, outlines of two feet side by side pointing in the same direction. Avner Goren collected photographs of these, so we recorded many for him. The Nabateans are not my own field of interest, but in the course of our explorations we saw and photographed many Nabatean inscriptions to aid the research of colleagues in the field. Eventually the photographs were incorporated into the database of the Rock Inscriptions and Graffiti Project that I established later; it is now (2016) mounted on the Internet and available to all (http://rockinscriptions.huji.ac.il).

On Rock VIII we suddenly found three Armenian letters. They were badly eroded, but careful later study revealed a fourth letter as well. We read them as "Mesr[op]," a personal name (H Arm 73).[4] Saint Mesrop was

---

4. Numbers such as this are used in publications of the inscriptions and in the database; see Michael E. Stone, *The Armenian Inscriptions from the Sinai with Appendixes on the Georgian and Latin Inscriptions by Michel van Esbroeck and William Adler*, Harvard Armenian Texts and Studies 6 (Cambridge: Harvard University Press, 1982).

2. THE FIRST EXPEDITION, 4–5 MARCH 1979

Fig. 4. Wadi Ḥajjaj, Rock III

the inventor of the Armenian alphabet at the start of the fifth century, and finding this name first signaled an auspicious beginning. We recorded, measured, and photographed the letters, then proceeded on to Rock III (fig. 4). This large rock has the most inscriptions of any in Wadi Ḥajjaj. Indeed, it is known as The Rock of Inscriptions. The Archaeological Staff Officer had a meter-high wall built around the base of the southern and eastern faces, which are covered with inscriptions. In this early afternoon hour, we started to examine Rock III from outside the wall. It did not take long for us to see the first of the Armenian inscriptions. With the permission of the bedouin caretaker employed by the Nature Reserves Authority, we clambered over the wall and started to study the rock more closely.

I immediately discerned an Armenian inscription that Negev did not record. It was the name Nathan, and as I looked at it shivers ran down my spine! It was old, so my instincts and everything I knew about Armenian writing told me, and not just old, but very old, going back to the first century of Armenian writing (H Arm 41). Remember that the Armenian alphabet was invented at the beginning of the fifth century. The oldest inscription known in 1979 when we started our work in the Sinai Peninsula was on a church in Tekor in present-day Turkey, and had been

---

H signifies Wadi Ḥajjaj and Arm that the inscription is in Armenian; 73 is the identifying number assigned to this inscription.

Fig. 5. At work in Wadi Ḥajjaj

written at the end of the fifth century. The next oldest inscription is in Armenia, and it was written in the year 618. Anything older than that is sensational. In a state of growing excitement, we worked around the rock and in short order discovered, photographed, and recorded eighteen Armenian inscriptions one after another as well as several in Georgian. The hunt was on! Not just to view the few inscriptions Negev had recorded but to find more.

At this early stage of the work, our eyes were not practiced in the difficult task of making out Armenian letters among the polyglot swarms of inscriptions on this rock. These inscriptions were sometimes written one on top of another, layer upon layer of writing in different languages (see fig. 6 below). We even observed one inscription in Ethiopic.[5] In addition, the Armenian inscriptions are usually quite small in size and generally short. Most of them merely give names. On the northeastern face of the rock, though, we found a number of inscriptions that later proved extremely important. One is a badly eroded inscription that originally contained about nine lines of writing. This is the longest of all the inscriptions we discovered in the Sinai (H Arm 42); this inscription, when studied in detail, yielded not only names but the words "Saint Cath/erine's" and "to pray," among others. Clearly, a pilgrim wrote it recording his experience. Another was, we thought at first, a particularly clear three-line inscription calling for the remembrance of a pilgrim and recording the name of the writer. When I studied it in detail back home, I discovered that it was in fact two separate inscriptions written by the same individual (H Arm 39–40). Our excitement increased as it became clear that this was a major find.

---

5. Eventually published by Émile Puech of the École Biblique in Jerusalem: "Une inscription éthiopienne ancienne au Sinaï (Wadi Hajjaj)," *Revue biblique* 87 (1980): 597–600.

2. THE FIRST EXPEDITION, 4–5 MARCH 1979

When we thought that we had finished work on Rock III, we proceeded to study the other rocks to the north of the road. We could not find the two Armenian inscriptions that Abraham Negev recorded from Rock II, but on its northern face, left of a curious rock formation, I observed an inscription in Syriac (a Christian Aramaic language). The day was passing, and we were eager to continue our search, so we moved on to Rocks V and VI. These are smaller than Rock III but still rather large, and they were located to the northwest of Rock III. Rock VI had nothing of interest to us, but as soon as we came to Rock V things changed dramatically (fig. 5).

We started at the southwestern corner of Rock V, and there once more we found inscriptions in Armenian and Georgian. This rock has far fewer inscriptions on it than does Rock III, but we immediately found nine Armenian inscriptions scattered all around it. One of these really brought things to a satisfactory climax: it read "I have gone around Moses," that is, "I have completed a circuit of Mount Moses [i.e., Jebel Musa]" (H Arm 71). A pilgrim wrote it triumphantly on his way back from a visit to Mount Sinai.

When were the inscriptions written? One of the Rock V inscriptions proved important for dating. An inscription in a square Arabic script had been engraved on top of it (H Arm 66). There was no doubt that the Arabic had been written after the Armenian. Later, in Jerusalem, Professor Moshe Sharon, an expert on Arabic epigraphy, confirmed to me that this sort of Arabic script was at the very latest of the ninth century. Thus the Armenian under it must be earlier. Another date emerged later from the study of one of the Rock III inscriptions; H Arm 56 contains the date 971 CE, and that inscription is, judging from the style of writing, one of the later inscriptions. Thus one immediate outcome of this first day's work was that we could fix the time of the inscriptions to the Byzantine and early Arab periods.

At that stage there was no doubt in our minds that we had to date the Armenian inscriptions from the fifth or sixth century on. They show that pilgrim traffic was active through this area until the tenth century or later.[6]

Thus the initial find already more than justified our visit. We had thought we would see a few known inscriptions in Wadi Ḥajjaj. Instead, we discovered more than twenty, including some new ones, two of which enabled us to determine dates. We searched for Negev's Site IX and could

---

6. Abraham Negev, *The Inscriptions of Wadi Haggag, Sinai*, Qedem 6 (Jerusalem: Institute of Archaeology, 1977), 77. Today scholars would put the end of Nabatean writing somewhat later, perhaps in the early fifth century.

not find it. Then we crossed the road and carefully examined Rocks IV and I, which are to the south of the road. Rock IV, small and about 150 meters west of Rock I, yielded no inscriptions at all. Rock I, however, is enormous, the largest *hadbe* of Wadi Ḥajjaj, and it took some time to survey it carefully because of its size. We found Georgian inscriptions that Negev had discovered there previously, as well as Greek and Nabatean ones. No Armenian, however, turned up; it seems that my pilgrims confined their attention to Rocks III, V, and VIII.

By now it was about 4:00 in the afternoon. A driver of the Neot Hakikar tours, an Israeli company conducting desert tours in special desert vehicles, told Uzi that someone had seen some strange inscriptions at Jebel Baraqa, which is about 12 kilometers south of Wadi Ḥajjaj. They were on the southeastern face of a sandstone hill, so we set off to find this site. The going was rough; there were no roads, and on two occasions Uzi had to stop and let some air out of the jeep's tires to increase their purchase in the sand.

The first wadi through which we attempted to travel proved to be blocked with stones and impassable even for a jeep. A second attempt took us in a larger circle around the blocked wadi, and we managed to reach the site. There we found the rock without difficulty. On the smooth rock face were some delicate drawings and three inscriptions in what looked to us like Aramaic. We thought that what we had found were three old inscriptions in Jewish Aramaic. This was exciting; we had also seen one or two Jewish inscriptions on Rock III at Wadi Ḥajjaj. However, later my colleague, the great Hebrew epigrapher Professor Joseph Naveh pointed out that the three inscriptions we had found on Jebel Baraqa were in fact Nabatean. The type of Nabatean script used in them is quite similar to older forms of the square Hebrew or Aramaic script (the "ordinary" Hebrew script). This shows their age, and they may be among the oldest Nabatean inscriptions known. They were all three written by the same man, and later we found another inscription by him in Wadi Mukattab, on the other, western, side of the desert. In the twilight of that first day's work in the Sinai, however, I did not know all this. Instead, I photographed the inscriptions as well as I could in the fading light, then the rock drawings. I could not decipher the inscriptions; the script was not immediately transparent, and in any case it was nearly dark.

On the way to Jebel Baraqa, Uzi had taken us to see one of the famous sites of the Sinai, the *nawamis*. We drove to an area of flat ground covered with pieces of brittle, reddish-brown sandstone. We parked the jeep and started to walk across the flat rocky area to a ridge of rock ahead. The stone squeaked and cracked as we crushed it under foot, with a sound that seemed to echo the dryness of the area. We sat on the ridge amazed at the acute silence.

Then Uzi pointed out a group of about forty round stone structures a hundred meters before us. These *nawamis* are circular, with doors on the west and flat roofs. They looked like a collection of hatboxes with oblongs cut out of one side. The masonry was all flakes of local sandstone with large rocks forming the lintels. The *nawamis* are ancient tombs, probably of the fifth–fourth millennium BCE; it was a strange walk over the crunching rock and through this village of hatboxes of the dead. The name means "mosquitoes," and the bedouin relate that they were built by the Israelites exiting Egypt as protection against the mosquitoes with which God punished them. These are not the only *nawamis* in the Sinai, and twenty-two other such sites are known. The Sinai travelers often discussed these remarkable monuments.

From Jebel Baraqa we set out in northerly direction toward the road. I was amazed at Uzi's navigational skills, for we drove most of that way through unmarked desert in the dark; as far as I recall, he did not stop once for purposes of orientation. We reached the road at Wadi Ḥajjaj and drove for about three quarters of an hour to our guesthouse in Nweiba. We were glad enough for hot showers, hot meals, and comfortable beds. The place seemed pleasant, but we did not see much of it. Our room charges included breakfast. Since we planned to leave early, we asked the staff there to prepare breakfast in advance. Before going to sleep, Tom and I spent some time discussing possible interpretations of the inscriptions we had found. We wanted to isolate problems so as to use our remaining time as profitably as possible, particularly to review our interpretation of some difficult inscriptions.

I remarked before that I did most of the photography myself. This posed its challenges. Fortunately, many of the inscriptions were within easy reach from the ground. These I could photograph without much difficulty. To get to some I had to climb up on the wall around Rock III; on other occasions I stood on the jeep. One suggestion we had been given was that the inscriptions would be clearer when dampened. Uzi had brought a small spray bottle with him to dampen them with water. This got us into trouble with the bedouin watchman who told us off roughly, although in fact this does not damage the inscriptions at all. In the end, I was not convinced that the spraying helped, and I did without it on later expeditions.

What made most difference to the photographs was the lighting. The inscriptions are shallow, and the play of light and shade is essential even to find them. Each time we examined a rock at a different time of day we found new inscriptions, for the light came at different angles. The rock's surface is also less than even, having many different facets and making it crucial to take a series of photographs at different times of the day. Certain incised lines only became visible as the light changed. I tried using a flash with a long extension cord as well, holding it at different angles so we could vary the light on the inscriptions; this technique produced good results on some occasions. All this work, I should remark, was done with black and white film. I had chosen very slow film because it produces the highest resolution images and could easily be used in the blinding light of the desert. On later trips I brought two camera bodies, one with black and white film and one with 35mm color film—black and white for inscriptions and rock drawings; color for 35 mm slides of the scenery.

Monday, 5 March 1979

On Monday morning the false dawn saw us up and off with the least possible delay. Our plan was to reach Wadi Ḥajjaj with the first light. This would

Fig. 6. Superimposed inscriptions and crosses, Rock III at Wadi Ḥajjaj

guarantee the side lighting that is helpful both for finding and for photographing inscriptions. When we reached Wadi Ḥajjaj, we headed directly for Rock III. I wanted to photograph inscriptions on the eastern side of that rock that had been in the dark the previous day. The early morning light came, of course, from the east. I took these photographs, then proceeded to work systematically around this rock, listing the inscriptions anew and checking some of the queries that Tom and I had discussed the preceding evening. As we proceeded with this task, we started to discover even more new inscriptions; by the time we finished, the total number was well over twenty on Rock III alone.

Having examined this rock as carefully as we could—though not carefully enough, as we later discovered—we went on to Rock V. I studied this rock in the same way I had done to Rock III: reexamining all the inscriptions, rephotographing some of them, and making more notes. Here we discovered nothing new, unlike at Rock III. This is because Rock III is crowded with such a mass of inscriptions, some superimposed one on the other, that it is impossible to see everything on one, two, or even three examinations (fig. 6).

During our expeditions I must have examined the inscribed parts of the rock carefully half a dozen times, and on each occasion I discovered new inscriptions. Rock V is much more even, however, and the inscriptions are well spaced out, so that it is much easier to find them, and I believe we exhausted all its offerings.

SINAI SCENES 3
Wind-shaped round sandstone marbles on a rocky shelf,
Wind-carved monstrous rocks,
pitted, rounded, irregular crevices,
Drawings, writing, and
low down—bedouin signs.

MES

After resurveying these two rocks, we decided to try once again to find Negev's Site IX. As before, this search proved to be in vain: we did not find it. By now it was well on into the morning, so we ate some breakfast and/or lunch (brunch sounds a bit upscale for it) in the shade of some rocks. We had finished our work at Wadi Ḥajjaj, or so we thought. We still planned to do several things. The first was to go to Wadi Arade, a wadi that runs off the road roughly to the north about 10 kilometers west of Wadi Ḥajjaj. We wished to see a particularly rich collection of petroglyphs (rock drawings) that covered the face of a rock to the eastern side of the wadi. Innumerable camels and riders decorated it, and some scenes of hunting were magnificently executed. One, for example, portrays two men capturing an ostrich by means of some sort of ropes attached to its legs. The ostrich is now extinct in the Sinai but was known there up to the beginning of the twentieth century. There was also one Nabatean inscription. We examined the drawings carefully, then checked other parts of the wadi in the vicinity in order to see whether there were any inscriptions of interest to us there. There was a drawing of an Egyptian boat but no more inscriptions, so we turned back.

Our limitation was that we had to reach Eilat in time to return the jeep and catch our plane out in late afternoon. We wished, however, to visit the oasis of 'Ein Fortaga to the east and north of Wadi Ḥajjaj. It was possible that this had been a pilgrim station. When we arrived there, the oasis impressed us greatly, for it is in a valley with steep sides that are of metamorphic rock and granite, giving a feeling of closing us in. In this oasis there are palm trees and other vegetation. There was not a great deal of water flowing, since for some time a drought had afflicted the Sinai, causing the water level to drop. It was, nonetheless, an impressive setting, and we made coffee and rested by a pool that in better years would have been a fine swimming hole. There were no inscriptions there, however—a fact that Abraham Negev had noted and we now verified. He had attributed the absence of inscriptions to the granite rock in that area. However, our later investigations elsewhere showed that there are regions of granite rocks where inscriptions abound. This visit to 'Ein Fortaga was our first attempt to investigate the routes taken by the pilgrims who left their mark in Wadi Ḥajjaj. We knew that one route entered the desert from Eilat (ancient Aila), but the exact paths followed between Eilat and Wadi Ḥajjaj remained unknown.

From 'Ein Fortaga we started back to Eilat. We punctured a tire on the way and had to change wheels at the petrol station in Nweiba. This did not daunt us, and we reached Eilat in plenty of time for our plane. I spent the last half-hour in the airport with Uzi discussing the possible implications of this extraordinary set of findings. We had discovered forty Armenian inscriptions and perhaps nine Georgian ones. It was clear to me that we had to return to the Sinai to continue the search.

2. THE FIRST EXPEDITION, 4–5 MARCH 1979

A few days later I left for Philadelphia. I had earlier undertaken to organize a workshop on Armenian paleography and epigraphy for the University of Pennsylvania. This was before my new discoveries in the Sinai. It turned out to be a nice coincidence: a workshop on Armenian epigraphy and newly found, very ancient Armenian inscriptions to show off there.

In Philadelphia I received support and funding for my next two visits to the Sinai. The Tarzian Chair for Armenian History and Culture of the University of Pennsylvania most kindly granted me a sum of money to support the coming expeditions and covered many of the expenses incurred on this first visit. However, the next trip had to await my return from the United States. In the meanwhile, I was able to work through the inscriptions that I had photographed and form a good idea not only of what they said but also some of the difficulties they raised. Beyond anything else, the number of inscriptions and the volume of the pilgrim traffic to which they bore witness astounded me. Moreover, my familiarity with Armenian inscriptions in general convinced me that these inscriptions belonged to the earliest stratum of Armenian epigraphical evidence.

While I was in Philadelphia I had occasion to discuss the Sinai find with Philip Mayerson of New York University, an expert on the history of the Sinai Peninsula and the Negev Desert. I also showed photographs of the inscriptions to scholars of Armenian. The outcome of the interchanges was to confirm my view of the antiquity of the inscriptions. News of the inscriptions also reached the American Armenian press. All this encouraged me to pursue the matter. On my return to Israel in early April, I spoke with Avner Goren, the Staff Officer for antiquities. My first aim, arising out of my rushed consultation with Uzi in the Eilat airport, was to check out the chief routes of pilgrimage in western Sinai, including the famed Wadi Mukattab. For this I needed the cooperation of Avner and his staff, who were located at the Sinai administration center near Saint Catherine's Monastery. I proceeded to try to carry out as much as possible of the plan Uzi and I had drawn up in that hurried half-hour, still in shock at the wealth and antiquity of the Wadi Ḥajjaj finds.

The two months between expeditions also gave me time to set up a method of reference, make draft decipherments, and read whatever I could find about the Armenians in the Sinai. A series of problems had arisen in the study of the new inscriptions that made it imperative for us to return to Wadi Ḥajjaj. These problems had to do partly with decipherment. As I indicated, photography was challenging, and many inscriptions were lightly incised and partly effaced, so there were still open queries about the actual decipherment. In addition, the wealth of the Wadi Ḥajjaj find raised the further question of the routes the pilgrims traveled from Jerusalem and the other sites in the heart of Israel to the Sinai. A substantial part of the answer to this question was to be found in the wadis and inscriptions of the Sinai.

3
The Second Expedition
9–17 May 1979

Wednesday, 9 May 1979

Our interest in tracing pilgrim routes led us to consider other groups of inscriptions in the Sinai. Wadi Mukattab, "the Inscribed Wadi," is a region in western Sinai containing a concentration of inscriptions, on the main route from the Gulf of Suez to Saint Catherine's Monastery from the west. We had high hopes of finding substantial numbers of Armenian inscriptions there. Ancient pilgrims often used this route, as we learn from their reports.

In the nineteenth century Arthur Penrhyn Stanley remarked on the easy access to the Nabatean inscriptions of Wadi Mukattab, even of those quite a way off the ground. This is quite accurate, but what is not true is his comment that their numbers were greatly exaggerated. The overall number of inscriptions in Wadi Mukattab had been discussed for 150 years, and in the end we could confirm that they numbered in the thousands.[1]

My attention had also been drawn to Wadi Leja, which is also called Wadi El-Arba'in, or Wadi of the Forty, after the small Monastery of the Forty Martyrs situated within it. It is close by Saint Catherine's Monastery and is a subsidiary house and orchard of that great institution. Julius Euting in his book on Nabatean inscriptions from the Sinai transcribed an Armenian inscription from this area with the notation "undeutlich," meaning "unclear." Although he did not recognize the language, he made a clear copy.[2]

---

   1. The Rock Inscriptions Project database, which is far from a complete documentation of this wadi, lists 1,063 inscriptions there.
   2. Julius Euting, *Sinaïtische Inschriften* (Berlin: Reimer, 1891), 9 (inscription 45[a]) and plate 3.

Tom and I took the early flight to Eilat, leaving Jerusalem at 8:00 AM, which meant being at the airline terminal at 7:00 AM. The airlines had been grounded by a strike, which ended just before we departed. That complicated our arrangements: due to the airlines' changes in scheduling, we had to leave a day earlier, and instead of flying directly to Saint Catherine's, we were to fly to Eilat, meet Uzi, and be picked up from Eilat by jeep. Our principal aim was to follow up our exciting find in Wadi Ḥajjaj and to see whether there were as many Armenian inscriptions at the chief known sites of western Sinai as we had found in eastern Sinai. Although this was the main purpose of our trip, the change in our plans, we hoped, would enable us to revisit Wadi Ḥajjaj on the way from Eilat to Saint Catherine's.

Uzi met us at the airport in Eilat, and we went to his house to await the jeep from Saint Catherine's with its bedouin driver, Fatḥi. We were at Uzi's shortly after 9:00 AM but could not find Fatḥi. He turned up a couple of hours later; the jeep had broken down somewhere south of Nweiba, which forced him to sleep out next to the jeep, then fix it and drive to Eilat. At the same time the Motorola, as the radio transceiver is commonly called, needed repair, so Fatḥi had to go to the Motorola agency to see about it. This also took some time, and in the end it was not repaired for our trip. Because of all this, it was already early afternoon when we set out: Fatḥi at the wheel, Uzi, Tom, and me.

Fatḥi was a young man belonging to the bedouin tribe who live in the Saint Catherine's area. He worked some years with Avner Goren, the archaeological officer for the Sinai, whose headquarters were at the administration complex near Saint Catherine's. Fatḥi was a most delightful person to whom we became increasingly attached as the days went past. He showed a great interest in our studies and work and took an active part in all our searches. His Hebrew was excellent, for which I was grateful, for I cannot speak his native Arabic.

The Mount Sinai bedouin, called the Jebaliyeh (People of the Mountain), are descended from a hundred slaves sent by the emperor Justinian to serve the monks. The slaves were from the Wallachian region of Romania, and in the course of the centuries they intermarried with the bedouin and converted to Islam.[3] They have traditional duties to the monks

---

3. Their relationship with other Sinai bedouin is briefly discussed by Burton Bernstein, *Sinai: The Great and Terrible Wilderness* (New York: Viking: 1979), 119; see also http://tinyurl.com/SBL9024a. John Galey gives striking images of bedouin life in *Sinai and the Monastery of St. Catherine* (Givatayim, Israel: Massada, 1980).

3. THE SECOND EXPEDITION, 9–17 MAY 1979

and also are by right recipients of certain bounties from the monastery. Burckhardt's travel record from the early nineteenth century speaks of considerable tensions between the bedouin and the monks.[4] The balance of power between the monks and the bedouin varied from time to time, and the existence of a mosque within the monastery walls witnesses to a time when the bedouin were dominant.

The jeep, which was not in very good condition, caused continuous problems. It overheated, and the fuel line kept clogging. Thus we were unable to take full advantage of this versatile vehicle. The rented jeeps that we used on our first expedition, and again on our third expedition, were in much better condition. However, Avner Goren had been kind enough to put the jeep with Fathi as driver at our disposal for the duration of our mission, for which we were more than grateful. The jeep is the major expense in these expeditions, and having the opportunity to meet Fathi made it all worthwhile.

The road down to Wadi Ḥajjaj was as scenic as we had remembered it, but the delay in leaving Eilat meant that we had only a short time to spend there. As a result, it was impossible to do what I had desired, which was to survey all the rocks and cliffs of this area systematically. In the course of an hour or so, we turned up three new Armenian inscriptions on the same Rock III that had previously yielded the bulk of material. In addition to discovering these new inscriptions, we were able to reexamine a number of previously known inscriptions and to resolve queries that had arisen in the course of study of the notes and photographs from our first visit.

The brief visit to Wadi Ḥajjaj was quite fruitful, but I was excited and impatient. I wanted to get on with the east Sinai survey. The magnitude of the find and the limits to our resources combined to produce an acute sense of urgency.

From Wadi Ḥajjaj to Saint Catherine's we traveled along the usual route, which is by Bir Sa'al (the word *bir* means "well"). After the Wadi Sa'al turn off, the road passes through mountainous country, and the route that one travels is along the wadi itself.

Throughout the part of the Sinai we surveyed, wadis (valleys) are the arteries of travel. Their beds may be quite narrow or wide, and most often rocky cliffs of varying height bound them on both sides. The travel routes

---

4. John Lewis Burckhardt, *Travels in Syria and the Holy Land* (London: Murray, 1822), 554–56. Burckhardt discusses the origins of the Mount Sinai bedouin on 562–65.

themselves are sandy or stony paths that run along the lower parts of the wadis. In many cases a path does not run along the actual floor or bed of the wadi but along one side, at a greater or lesser elevation from the ground. Some wadis are well traveled; in others there is scarcely any traffic. Naturally, even a jeep cannot drive through every area that a camel or a traveler on foot can traverse, and sometimes we were forced to abandon a particular route because it was impassable for us, although not for camels or donkeys. We noted such places and planned to survey them on camels. However, the events that unfolded frustrated that plan.

The major wadis are the highways of the desert and determine the flow of human traffic. This fact made our survey possible, for the routes and passages imposed by the configuration of the land have not changed over the centuries. The wadis have no running water, although some of them have water sources, such as 'Ein Fortaga, which we had previously visited. However, when the very rare rains do fall, powerful flash floods torrent down the wadis. This may explain why travelers were reluctant to use the relatively easy wadi bed for travel but instead elected to travel some distance up a wadi's sides.

Saint Catherine's Monastery (fig. 7) is about an hour's drive past Wadi Ḥajjaj, and on the way we passed the mouth of Wadi Arade with its remarkable rock drawings. The area as a whole is quite mountainous, and the mountains are high, granite, and very imposing. As already mentioned, Jebel Katerina (or Mount Catherine) and Jebel Musa (or Mount Moses, i.e., Mount Sinai) are among the highest. In fact, Mount Catherine at 2,629 meters is the highest peak in the Sinai. These adjoining peaks dominate the level area of Saint Catherine's at their foot, where the administration was located.

The administration housed a number of different institutions.[5] The most famous, of course, was Saint Catherine's Monastery at the foot of Jebel Musa, which many visitors have described and which we visited later on.[6] The Byzantine emperor Justinian constructed Saint Catherine's Monastery, a fortress-like building, between 548 and 565 CE. Great mosaics decorate the interior of its basilical church, a famous one being the transfiguration of Christ installed over the apse. The ancient church building

---

5. At the time of our expedition the area was administered by Israel; it reverted to Egyptian administration in November 1979.

6. Descriptions are too numerous to set forth. A fine set of pictures may be found in Galey's *Sinai and the Monastery*.

3. THE SECOND EXPEDITION, 9–17 MAY 1979

also incorporates the later Chapel of the Burning Bush, which is associated with Moses's bush. We saw a bush there that the monks claimed was a scion of Moses's original one. That was one of the chief attractions for pilgrims coming to this area. Egeria, the intrepid fifth-century nun from Spain, wrote: "the bush (which is still alive and sprouting) ... is the Burning Bush out of which the Lord spoke to Moses." The bush I saw a millennium and a half later is a bramble (*Rubus sanctus*), as thorny as a blackberry but lighter green in color.

Saint Catherine's is a Greek Orthodox monastery and has been in continuous use since its foundation in the sixth century (fig. 7). The bishop lives in Cairo, and over the years the monastery has developed a close relationship with the Greek Patriarchate of Jerusalem. Monks live not only in the monastery itself but also in cells and caves in the surrounding mountains. To this day there are some ascetic monks living in caves whose food is brought regularly from the monastery. This was the pattern of monasti-

Fig. 7. Greek map of Saint Catherine's Monastery and region

cism in Sinai before Justinian had the fortress-monastery built, and we know of monks there from the earliest days of Christian monasticism living a solitary and eremitic life. Today the monks are mainly Greeks, and most serve in Saint Catherine's Monastery for a limited period of time.

The airfield built by the Israeli Sinai Administration was about 2 kilometers to the north of Saint Catherine's. It greatly facilitated travel both for tourists and for those going down to the Sinai for research purposes. The Israeli Sinai Development Administration was located a couple of kilometers south of the monastery. They had an excellent clinic staffed by a doctor and nurses to serve the local population, and there were some other civilian administrative personnel as well. There was also a field school not far from the administration dwellings. Field schools are maintained by the Israel Nature Protection Society as research and educational centers. The Saint Catherine's Field School provided services, guidance, and information about this remarkable area to groups of visitors and young people. The young men and women working at the field school were deeply familiar with the region. They had hiked all over the area and did a wonderful job in helping people to experience the desert, while making every effort to prevent visitors from doing it any damage. This was also the task of the government's Nature Reserves Authority, which had a branch there. In short, there was a fair amount of building, but like all the building done under Israeli auspices in the Sinai, the structures were low and made of undressed local stone, so that they fit in admirably with the landscape.

As I continued working in the Sinai, I found this sensitivity to the desert ecology to be a most remarkable dimension of the administration. A love for the desert permeated all the officials whom I encountered. The low, rough-finished stone buildings, the use of solar power where feasible, and the attempt to impinge upon the desert as little as possible were praiseworthy. Neil Folberg, who visited Sinai again after the Israeli withdrawal, something I have never done, mourned the loss of this sensitivity in moving words. I have never returned because the research I left unfinished requires much off-road travel, which the Egyptian authorities forbid, as they do any other Israeli research. I was also apprehensive about their development of these areas and the sacrifice of local beauty. Now, as I write in 2016, the security situation in the Sinai is so grave, with the activity of Islamic militant groups against the Egyptian army, that any Israeli research is out of the question.

In the Saint Catherine's area, behind the administration buildings and trailing up the foot of a mountain, is the bedouin village. In addition to

3. THE SECOND EXPEDITION, 9–17 MAY 1979

their duties at the monastery, some of the bedouin, like Fathi, also worked for the Israeli administration. A school, one of a number we saw throughout the Sinai, had also been built close by the administration buildings.

By the end of our travel day we were comfortably settled in Avner Goren's spacious quarters, which he had put at our disposal. Avner's wife and children had lived there for some years, but when the children came of school age they returned to the north with their mother. It was now a bachelor's apartment full of archaeological supplies and implements, maps, and the like.

Thursday, 19 May 1979

On Thursday morning we hoped to embark on our way. However, Fathi wanted to get the jeep checked out, which took nearly all morning, and we almost had lunch at Saint Catherine's, too. Uzi had warned me in advance about "Sinai time." The difficulties of logistics, the distance from Eilat, not to speak of points further north, demands a slow pace. If it takes a long time to do something, that is just inevitable. One must accept it, and it does not help to chafe at the bit. Some things cannot be hurried; they work on Sinai time. Our jeep took hours to fix, and we had to adjust to that, but it was hard for me! The people who lived and worked at Santa, as they called it, loved the place with all their hearts. They all worked extremely hard under trying conditions, yet the atmosphere was intimate, calm, and imbued with a feeling of remoteness from urban settlement. Perhaps this very remoteness made it possible to relax. The majesty of the mountains and the depth of the sky put things into a special perspective. The north, with its cities, politics, and busyness, seemed far off, as it truly was. It would take a more lyrical pen than mine fully to capture the atmosphere of the place.

Since the jeep was not ready, we decided to walk to Wadi Leja nearby (fig. 8). The previous evening we had taken advantage of the last light to examine a number of rocks at the mouth of the wadi near the nunnery and the Nature Reserve Authority Station. We sought the Armenian inscription that Julius Euting had seen in Wadi Leja at the end of the nineteenth century. Inscriptions covered the rocks that we surveyed, but in the failing light we were not certain whether we saw Armenian or not. We were eager to get things underway, and this walk and search, which was on our agenda anyway, was a good release from our excitement.

So in the morning light we returned to the same area and examined these rocks. There were ample inscriptions, but none in Armenian. We

Fig. 8. The mouth of Wadi Leja: Jebel Safsafa on the left, Mount Catherine on the right, the administration buildings in the foreground

clambered several hundred meters into the wadi on the south side, where there is no path. We discovered nothing of significance there, nor did we find our inscription when we carefully examined the boulders lying before the wadi mouth. A little less than a kilometer into the wadi, below the spring and orchard that are in its midst, we did find Greek and Nabatean inscriptions and some crosses. At any rate, that was something.

Shortly before lunchtime, the jeep was ready and loaded with water, ample food, extra jerry cans of fuel, and our own equipment. Avner and Benny were both away when we arrived, but their assistant Shaul, together with Fathi, took excellent care of our every need. Supplies for us and all other necessities were ready. We took enough for three or four days in the field for the four of us. Fresh produce and dairy products had been ordered from the north by Avner's staff, and we picked them up at the airfield. This was a more luxurious expedition than others. We never took meat with us; Uzi told me that other researchers used to take meat to grill in the evenings. The books of desert travelers such as Wilfred Thresinger and Charles Doughty often contain tales of the bedouin slaughtering goats or even a camel for visitors. We were on a limited expedition with a distinct purpose and deliberately ate simple fare. To me, this seemed to be appropriate to the time and place: bread and cheese rather than roast goat. The

3. THE SECOND EXPEDITION, 9–17 MAY 1979

desert is a place where basic needs were foremost, and a complex cuisine would have felt out of place.

Our route took us through the Waṭiya Pass, about 20 kilometers north of our point of the administrative center. We observed inscriptions there in Arabic and Nabatean, but no Christian signs—either crosses or writing. We drove through Wadi el-Sheikh, whose breadth Burckhardt characterized as "noble," and into Wadi Feiran.[7] My notes and memory record nothing of the scenery on this route; all my thoughts were directed toward the inscriptions we hoped to find in Wadi Mukattab. More's the pity, since all the descriptions I have read describe Wadi el-Sheikh as a most impressive valley, one of the stateliest in southwestern Sinai.

Wadi Feiran, which is a continuation of Wadi el-Sheikh, is the largest oasis in the Sinai. The road winds through the thousands of date palms that grow in this area. High mountains tower over the oasis, the best known being Jebel Serbal to the south, which is 2,070 meters high. Later, in the last days before the Israeli withdrawal from that part of the Sinai, Uzi led a small expedition to Jebel Serbal and discovered a Nabatean temple on its peak.[8] In Wadi Feiran, there is a tell (artificial mound) with considerable remains of a Nabatean-Byzantine town that might hold some of the answers to the mysteries of the Nabatean presence in the Sinai. Many ancient sources refer to the city in Wadi Feiran.

This oasis was traditionally identified with Rephidim, where the people of Israel fought Amalek (Exod 17); in Byzantine times it was the seat of an episcopal see and a monastic establishment. In Feiran, too, a modest complex of buildings forming a bedouin center has been constructed. There is a garage, a school, a coffee house, a shop, and various administrative offices, all built by the local bedouin. The style of the building fitted with that encouraged under the Israeli administration. The Archaeological Officer had a storage facility at this Feiran center, and we picked up provisions there, particularly tinned goods.

---

7. Burckhardt, *Travels in Syria*, 599.

8. About inscriptions on Jebel Serbal, Stanley remarks, "it is difficult to reconcile the 'three inscriptions' which we saw, with the 'many' described by him [Burckhardt]" (*Sinai and Palestine*, 72; see Burckhardt, *Travels in Syria*, 604–9). Yet Stanley's remark is strange. The Rock Inscriptions Project database holds photographs of 793 inscriptions from Jebel Serbal. It seems that Stanley's mind was so focused on finding the desert stations of the wandering Israelites that his other observations were somewhat by the way.

Despite the numerous points of interest in Wadi Feiran, this time we did not stop there but rather, after collecting our supplies, pressed on. We had decided to drive directly to the most distant point planned for this expedition. Our general direction was westward, our destination being Wadi Maghara, meaning "Wadi of the Caves," quite a way on. Benny, Avner Goren's assistant, had many weeks before told me of an Armenian inscription at this spot. Although Wadi Mukattab with its

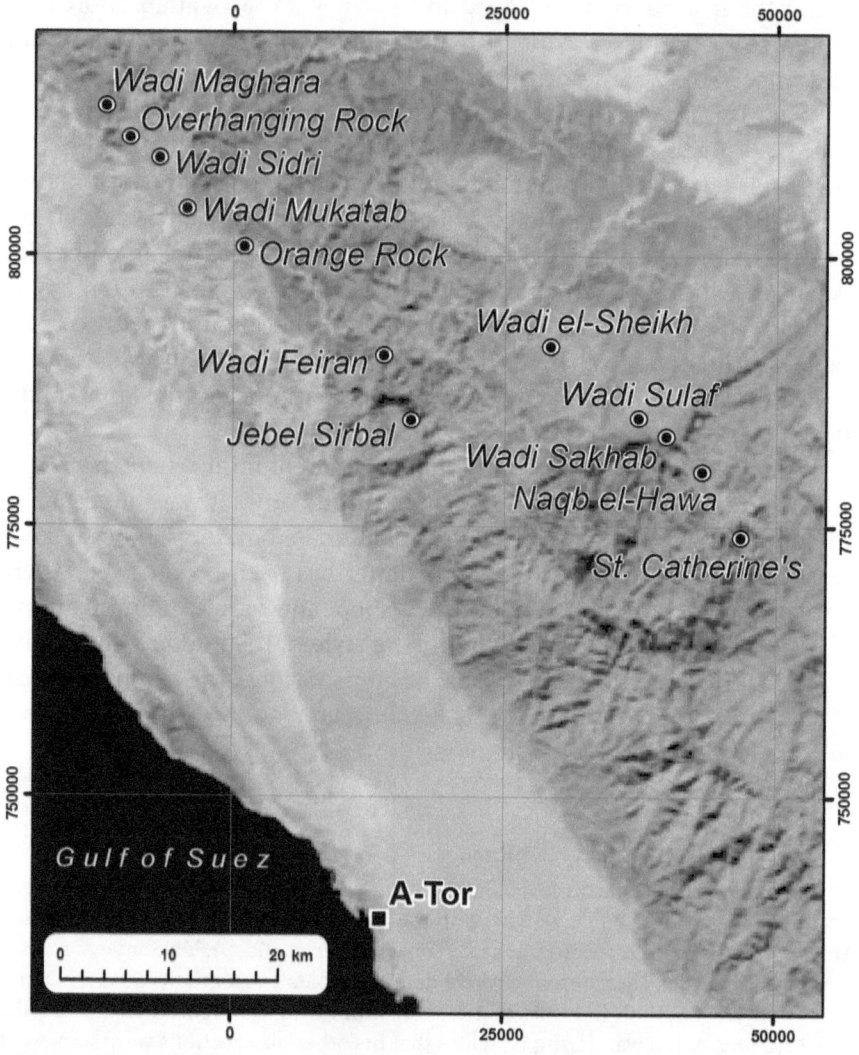

Map 3. Wadi Maghara to Saint Catherine's Monastery

3. THE SECOND EXPEDITION, 9–17 MAY 1979

Fig. 9. Tom and Uzi examine the overhanging rock, Wadi Maghara; bedouin mother and child in background

numerous inscriptions was the primary object of our journey, our first stop was beyond it.

To reach Wadi Maghara, we traversed a series of connecting wadis running roughly west from Naqb el-Hawa, which is 20 kilometers or so north of Santa Katerina. The wadis form a major way of travel from Egypt and the Gulf of Suez to Saint Catherine's Monastery and have been popular among pilgrims since antiquity. Traveling from east to west, these are Wadi el-Sheikh running into Wadi Feiran to Wadi Mukattab and then Wadi Sidri. We were aiming for the point at which Wadi Maghara runs into Wadi Sidri from the northeast. Wadi Sidri is the last wadi of this network that we traveled, although this major route continues west as far as Egypt, in Africa.

At the mouth of the wadi, a bedouin girl stopped us and more or less demanded some bread, water, and other food from us.[9] In general, the

---

9. In the early nineteenth century Burkhardt related the following similar incident: "In the midst of this desert we met a poor Bedouin woman, who begged some water of us; she was going to Akaba, where the tents of her family were, but had neither provisions nor water with her, relying entirely on the hospitality of the Arabs she

practice of hospitality is such that one always gives a lift to bedouin or others when possible, and on nearly every occasion when we visited a bedouin encampment they offered us something to drink. On the previous day we had brought a bedouin from Nweiba to a point not far from Wadi Ḥajjaj. Over and again someone would stop us in what seemed like total desert, would climb aboard, and then some time later would ask to be let off in a place as deserted in our eyes as the spot where he or she had mounted the jeep.

Perhaps a hundred yards inside Wadi Maghara, on the western side, we sighted a striking, large sandstone boulder prominently projecting into the wadi. It had a slanting overhanging face that cast a fine shadow in which a hot and tired traveler could rest (fig. 9).

SINAI SCENES 4
It is silent and still
daytime's heat
a palpable presence.
Quiet to rest in rock's shade.

MES

On the surface of this overhang we saw an extraordinary assortment of writing, reflecting the variety of people who had rested under this rock shelf. First the Armenian inscription, a single word in a fairly late style of writing, demanded our attention. There were also prominent inscriptions in Russian and Latin, the latter, dated 1850, reading *Deus salvatum fac Regem nostrum imperatoremque Nicolas I,* that is, God save our king and emperor Nicholas I (1825–1855). The Russian, Tom assured me, was of the same date and content. Russian pilgrimage was a widespread movement, and even those of modest means used to save for many years in order to make a trip to the holy places. This particular pilgrim knew Latin as well as Russian. On the same rock we also observed old Arabic inscriptions and some Egyptian hieroglyphs as well as some Old North Arabic, a form

---

might meet on the road…. She seemed to be as unconcerned, as if she were merely taking a walk for pleasure" (*Travels in Syria,* 448).

3. THE SECOND EXPEDITION, 9–17 MAY 1979

of writing used before the evolution of Nabatean into the current Arabic script (fig. 10).

On the other side of the wadi was the dwelling of the bedouin responsible for the area, working for the Nature Reserves Authority. He invited us for tea, and we spent a pleasant half hour there. From him we learned of various inscriptions in the area. About a hundred yards or so beyond the rock on which we had already seen inscriptions, a wadi branches off Wadi Maghara. More specifically, Wadi Maghara bears to the right and this branch, known as Wadi Iqna, to the left. Straight ahead is a high rocky cliff. Under the guidance of the bedouin, we followed the course of Wadi Maghara, and not far after the junction with Wadi Iqna, we saw on our left a high cliff face with numerous inscriptions in Nabatean and Greek as well as some rock drawings. We retraced our steps, followed by a crowd of bedouin children, and then, on the high rock cliff at the junction with Wadi Iqna we were shown two hieroglyphic inscriptions. This area was quite a center of mining activity in the ancient period, particularly of turquoise. There are still some of these turquoise stones around, for the bedouin children tried to sell us some. They kept them wrapped in cloths containing sand impregnated with olive oil. The oil penetrates the stones and enhances their color. Later, I was given to understand, it gradually dries

Fig. 10. Rock drawings and Nabatean inscription

out, and the color becomes lighter. I did not buy any stones on this visit, although I did so on my next trip there.

In the nineteenth century a Briton, Major C. K. MacDonald, not only visited the site but also resided there with his wife from 1857 to 1866. He is considered the first excavator of the Egyptian antiquities at Serabit el-Khadem, and he also made an effort to mine turquoise. He built himself a house of stone and palm beams a little further along Wadi Maghara. Eventually he despaired of the venture, left in 1866, and died in poverty in Cairo in 1870. It is rumored that he managed to destroy some hieroglyphic inscriptions over the main entrances with his blasting.[10]

We did not go as far as the mines, however, or to MacDonald's house. Near the hieroglyphic inscriptions at the mouth of Wadi Iqna, our bedouin host showed us a curious flat rock, perhaps 10 meters or less from the floor of the wadi. It had on it three large arrowheads, deeply cut, whose significance completely escaped us.

In this area we picked up some sherds and examined them, determining that they were of Middle Kingdom Egyptian provenance. The bedouin invited us to spend the night with them at the mouth of the wadi. They offered to bake bread for us and to extend their hospitality, but we were too eager to commence searching Wadi Mukattab, and there were still a few hours of light left. Therefore, we left the interesting Wadi Maghara. In retrospect, it is perhaps a pity that we felt so driven, for had we spent more time in this region and with its inhabitants, perhaps much of interest would have emerged.

At the entrance to Wadi Mukattab from this northwestern end, we observed two orange standing rocks. We stopped to examine them, for they were covered with inscriptions. They were on the southwestern side of the wadi, the side with the most inscriptions. As we examined them, Uzi suddenly called my attention to a single Georgian word enclosed within two crosses (M Georg 1). A little farther on, the inscriptions started in earnest, and the number of Nabatean inscriptions was enormous. There were fewer inscriptions in Greek but quite a lot in Arabic. We speculated why inscriptions concentrated chiefly on this side of the wadi. Perhaps it has

---

10. John D. Cooney writes, "Clearly, Macdonald was of a long line of British, male and female, who were intoxicated with the exotic civilizations of the East. Between them, they produced the world's greatest travel literature for they were for the most part well born, well educated, and exceptionally able with the pen" ("Major MacDonald, A Victorian Romantic," *Journal of Egyptian Archeology* 58 [1972]: 283).

more shade in the heat of the day. Not far past the Georgian inscription, I found another of the "Aramaic" inscriptions, or so we had wrongly dubbed them when we first found writing in this script in Jebel Baraqa. It was in the same style of archaic Nabatean as were the Jebel Baraqa inscriptions and written by the same person.

> SINAI SCENES 5
> They are all still there,
> Romans, Greeks, Nabateans,
> Armenians, Jews, Arabs,
> Bedouin, Sabeans, Egyptians.
> Layered human traffic of the wasteland.
>
> MES

We camped for the night not far from this point, on the southwestern side of the wadi. Our campsite was between cliffs covered with all sorts of inscriptions, and the next morning we discovered some Armenian writing just beyond where we had spent the night.

Darkness fell suddenly, so Uzi rigged a small light connected to the jeep battery, and we warmed some food, washed up, and laid out our sleeping gear—taking care to dig a hip hole in the sand, otherwise we would have been most uncomfortable. After food and drink, we extinguished the light. Fathi rolled up in his blanket and fell asleep at once—even at Santa Katerina, he preferred to sleep in the courtyard outside Avner's apartment, not inside. I walked a little distance up the "inlet" between the enclosing cliffs and tried to get a sense of the desert. The night was clear, absolutely still, and the heavens were extraordinarily brilliant, with no city light to dim the sky carpeted with stars. Later it grew chilly, and I was glad of the sleeping bag and its hood, as well as of a dram of brandy from my flask.

> SINAI SCENES 6
> Night's still cool,
> clarity and brilliance.

Always the quiet,
Where the voice can be heard,
If the ear is open.

The quiet is affirmation,
not sound's cessation,
to touch, to feel.
The soul responds to silence's solidity,
touchable.

MES

Friday, 21 May 1979

The next morning we awoke early, about 5:30, and after packing and eating breakfast we were soon on our way.

Sandstone cliffs line Wadi Mukattab. The soft stone is easy to work, and this was doubtless one of the reasons why so many inscriptions were written there. We had to survey this wadi on foot, so we split up and examined all the rocks on both sides. It is always possible to miss something, particularly among a plethora of inscriptions such as in Wadi Mukattab, but we were exceedingly careful, and the four of us (Fathi also took an active part in our search) did a pretty thorough search by any standard.

At the end of a rock cliff on the southwestern side of the wadi, we found an inscription in Latin (M Lat 2): FACTUS SENATUS ID PQ ROMANUS EX IMP....[11] The inscription is quite clear, except for the last word, but difficult to translate. It imitates Roman imperial formulas, but with mistakes. Later on Bill Adler, who also joined me on the fourth expedition, studied it. When he published the inscription, he noted that it seems to claim authority of the emperor by the words *ex imp*, which might mean "on the authority of the emperor."

Farther on another Latin inscription was observed: CESSENT SYRI ANTE LATINOS ROMANOS (M Lat 1).[12] I puzzled over this at the time,

---

11. The Sinai inscriptions mentioned in the course of this narrative can be viewed in the Rock Inscriptions and Graffiti Data Base at http://rockinscriptions.huji.ac.il/

12. Both Latin inscriptions are published in Stone, *Armenian Inscriptions from the Sinai*, "Appendix II: Latin Inscriptions," by William Adler, 183–86.

but later my colleague Abraham Wasserstein in Jerusalem suggested to me that "Syri" was a Latin Christian designation for the Greek Christians. If we read the inscription in this way, it calls for the Greeks to cede or give way before the Latin Roman Christians. However, the context of this summons is unclear. G. F. Grey published this Latin inscription in 1830, and many theories developed about it. These and the bilingual Russian and Latin inscription of 1850 in Wadi Maghara were the most intriguing Latin inscriptions we observed in the course of all our wanderings through the Sinai. They had apparently been written by individuals whose Latin was far from perfect.

Tom found the first of the Armenian inscriptions that day. It was scratched on the rock in a rather recent hand. Next, in a sort of niche or inlet in the rock, near a signpost erected by the Nature Reserves Authority, we found the six-line inscription that Benny had mentioned. It turned out to be Georgian, not Armenian (M Georg 2). It is fairly well preserved, but the ends of the lines and the lower part have eroded. Just by the Georgian inscription, on a flat stone, I found a single Armenian letter, all that time's decay had left of a longer inscription. Ten or fifteen yards northwest of the Georgian inscription Tom found another Armenian one, this time in minuscule letters—the only minuscule inscription in Wadi Mukattab. Nearly all the Armenian inscriptions of any period are written in majuscule, or capital, letters. Majuscules seem to have been the only letters the Armenian script had for several centuries. Small (minuscule) letters developed by the tenth century, probably somewhat earlier, but even after manuscripts and documents were written as a matter of course in minuscule letters, the Armenians continued to write inscriptions in majuscules; they usually do so down to the present day. This conservatism is equally true of English inscriptions, so often written in capital letters. Thus an Armenian inscription in minuscule is quite rare. We found only one other, at Wadi Ḥajjaj.

Farther down the wadi we discovered two more inscriptions in the archaic Nabatean script and, on the other side of the wadi, two Armenian letters that, by sheer luck, I spied from the jeep. These were all the Armenian inscriptions that we discovered in the areas west of Saint Catherine's. This is remarkable, particularly in view of the large number of inscriptions in Wadi Mukattab and the almost equally large number we found in Wadi Shellaleh on our next trip, which is even farther to the northwest than we had reached on this visit.

All of our exploration of Wadi Mukattab was over by 10:30 that Friday morning, 11 May 1979. We spent some time discussing what we should do and how we might most fruitfully spend the rest of the time we had at our disposal. We decided to retrace our tracks as far as Wadi Feiran. In this wadi, at the point at which Wadi Nisrin runs into it, there was, we had been told, a rock with a large number of inscriptions on it. We proceeded to explore this area, which indeed had numerous inscriptions. There were Nabatean and quite a number of Christian inscriptions there but not a letter of Armenian. By now we were somewhat dispirited. In this part of western Sinai we had expected to find a crop of inscriptions comparable to that we had found at Wadi Ḥajjaj. After all, so we had reasoned, we should find considerable numbers of Armenian inscriptions in the region that bore the greatest number of inscriptions in the whole Sinai Peninsula and that was on a commonly frequented pilgrimage route. Yet among all those inscriptions we had examined, only five Armenian inscriptions had been found. Of these, the ones that could be assigned approximate dates were all late. It was only as I considered the implications of this surprising discovery over the next two or three days that the hypotheses that guided our further work emerged.

For the moment we were in Wadi Feiran, some way past the point at which Wadi Nisrin runs into it. Uzi wished to leave us for a day, so he could climb the mountain called Jebel Moneijat Musa, or Mountain of Moses's Meeting with God. On this mountain was a Nabatean sanctuary. Uzi's plan was to climb up that evening, spend the night on the mountain, examine the sacred enclosure and the inscriptions, and descend the next day. We arranged for him to contact us the next day via radio from the bedouin center at Feiran. Then Fatḥi would set out from Saint Catherine's to pick him up.

We left Uzi with the minimal provisions that he took with him for this trip, basically water and dried figs. The figs are relatively lightweight and a good source of energy. Uzi spends much of his time in the desert and was deeply tanned and extremely fit. He is a desert archaeologist of great experience, and his knowledge was all-inclusive. He did not merely know the archaeology but was also deeply familiar with the flora and fauna, the terrain itself, its geology, and its history. He was fascinated by cult places and carried out extensive research on Chalcolithic period sites (mid-fifth to mid-fourth millennium BCE). Another great interest of his was Nabatean cult places. It was this interest, as well as the challenge of the mountain itself, that drove him to climb Jebel Moneijat Musa.

We returned to Saint Catherine's with Fatḥi, albeit via a rather long detour. Following the leads in one or two nineteenth-century travelers' reports, we set out to search for a certain Wadi Ber(r)a, which was supposed to harbor inscriptions. From Wadi Feiran we turned southwest into Wadi Sulaf and traveled as far as the area called Buwera, which is not far from Sheikh 'Awad, on the chief pilgrim way. After that the pilgrim route led through the pass named Naqb el-Hawa to the Saint Catherine's area (see map 2 above). We did not penetrate as far as Sheikh 'Awad, an omission we later regretted, for this short stretch from the area of Buwera to the northwestern end of Naqb el-Hawa remained unvisited by us. Since then we have received reports of Christian inscriptions at Sheikh 'Awad. Instead of going on the extra few kilometers, we returned by way of Wadi Sakhab, which runs more or less parallel to Wadi Sulaf and debouches into Wadi El-Sheikh.

If I look back at many events, especially in field work in the Sinai and in monasteries with manuscript collections, I see a personal flaw. I should have learned by now that, once in a place, one should photograph everything possible. Once traveling somewhere, take the extra bother, make the effort, and go on as far as possible. Over the years I missed some manuscripts I should have photographed, some inscriptions that should have been, as a photographer friend used to say "in the box." So, too, it was with Sheikh 'Awad. At the end of my Sinai work, I regretted not having made the extra effort on that day.

We did find some Arabic and Nabatean inscriptions in the area of Wadi Buwera, but again the Armenian was conspicuous by its absence. We returned to Saint Catherine's toward evening. Instead of proceeding to our rooms, we ran over to examine the boulders at the mouth of Wadi Leja once more. Euting's inscription was still bothering us, and we thought that perhaps the solution lay there. It was late, however, and the inscriptions on the granite surface were already invisible by the time we arrived.

Fathi dropped us off at the quarters we had used on our first night. It was Friday night, so instead of the usual light, dairy supper, we were guests as a full Sabbath meal served in the administration dining room. In honor of the Sabbath, there were candles, white tablecloths, and a pleasant repast. The people who work there are an interesting mixture. I talked with one or two old-timers, men in their seventies who had come down to the Sinai soon after 1967, when they retired from their previous jobs. They were lively and full of stories of the old days. Each one had family, children, and grandchildren in the north.

The others were young people, some couples and some single. They worked in all sorts of fields. A doctor and a nurse staffed the clinic serving the area. We were to see them in a day or two, as it happened. There were people working for the Nature Reserves Authority, automobile mechanics, administrative people, and so forth—a little community exhibiting great amity, at least on the surface. I suspect the amity was real, for the people who were drawn to live in this wild country were of singular characteristics. In the course of table talk at dinner, we were given some leads about possible concentrations of inscriptions in the area of Wadi Leja, and we were determined to make use of Saturday morning, solving the mystery of Euting's inscription.

Saturday, 12 May 1979

Tom and I set out by foot at what seemed to us to be a luxurious hour of 8:00 AM. Our aim was to transverse Wadi Leja, or as it was also called, Wadi el-Arba'in. This second name derives from the name of the monastery that lies in it, known as Deir el-Arba'in, Monastery of the Forty. I heard two stories about the name: the forty were either the forty martyrs of Sebastia or forty monks killed by bedouin marauders. The area around Jebel Katerina and Jebel Musa is dotted with holy places at which events mentioned in the Bible or the Qur'an supposedly took place. It was this sanctity that, in the final analysis, drew pilgrims and monks to the site.

We planned to enter Wadi Leja from its northwest end, which lies behind the Field School, and to explore until we came across Euting's inscription. Wadi Leja is one of the chief paths taken to the peak of Jebel Musa. Pilgrims entered this way, ascended Jebel Musa from Wadi Leja, and continued up the mountain to the Vale of Elijah. This wadi also provided an approach to Jebel Katerina. The inscriptions in this part of the wadi were Nabatean and were much farther into the wadi than we had gone on the previous Thursday morning. From this point on, however, Nabatean and Arabic inscriptions, but particularly the former, became more frequent. We also saw a number of crosses incised in the rock. Most of the inscriptions were beside the ancient path that had been paved by the monks, along which we were now proceeding.

The mountains on both sides of this wadi are quite high. The mountain on the northern side is part of the granite massif of Jebel Safsafa and Jebel Musa, commonly identified as Mount Horeb and Mount Sinai, respectively.

3. THE SECOND EXPEDITION, 9–17 MAY 1979

SINAI SCENES 7
Elijah hid on Horeb's height,
Catherine's body niche,
and Jethro's tomb on a hill.

Rephidim, Amalek,
the thorny bush and Miriam's well,
the monastery and a solitary's cave,
Byzantine paving.

MES

Huge granite boulders are strewn throughout the wadi; they become somewhat more frequent and larger closer to its mouth, where we entered. There is a water source about a kilometer in, so we went down to the stream and refreshed ourselves in the spring water. We drank the water—the spring and well water of the Sinai is not polluted and can be safely drunk. A black plastic pipe lay along the wadi bed, and at one place it had been punctured and a fountain of water shot up into the air about 3 m. This pipe brought water to Saint Catherine's Monastery, for the wells inside the monastery were polluted.

There were luxuriant fruit trees that the bedouin tended for the monks: pomegranates, almonds that were in fruit while we were there, and olives. Stone walls surrounded the orchards.[13] Part of the agreement between the bedouin and the monks was that the bedouin would cultivate these gardens, which flourished because of the abundant water source in the wadi. Not far from the bedouin cultivation, a new chapel was still in the course of construction. It commemorates, according to local tradition, the site of the stone from which Moses brought forth water. This tradition is ancient, and reports of the stone and its supposed twelve "mouths" for the twelve tribes of Israel feature in many a traveler's tale. As we approached this site, the number of inscriptions increased. There were increasingly more Christian ones, mostly in Greek and some in Arabic. The Nabatean, however, continued to predominate.

---

13. Burckhardt describes these orchards in the early nineteenth century (*Syria and the Holy Land*, 578); they do not seem to have changed much.

The first Armenian inscription we found in the area was on a rock to the right (i.e., the south) of the path, just by the chapel under construction. We photographed and recorded it and almost resolved to conclude our walk there and return. From there, however, we could see more inscribed rocks not far ahead; after these there were yet still more, and we were led by our curiosity from one to the next. It was good that we followed the prompting of our excitement, because about 500 meters beyond the chapel, the second Armenian inscription was spotted on a large, orange-tinted granite rock to the north of the path. This was the one that Euting had seen and recorded as "undeutlich" in the nineteenth century. It read "Jacob."[14] Indeed, by the prominence of its position and the size of its characters, this inscription made a ready impression on anyone who passed by. Thus in some measure the Jacob who incised his name saved himself from oblivion.

Tom discovered the third of the Armenian inscriptions we found on this morning, on the first of three large rocks to the south of the path, about 200 meters beyond the Jacob inscription. This inscription, reading "I saw Jerusalem," is a particularly important witness to the route followed by Armenian pilgrims (L Arm 3). We did not go much farther along Wadi Leja, for the inscriptions became less frequent, and we turned back from a point about 250 meters before the stone wall that marks the westernmost part of the monastery gardens. We walked back without delay and left the wadi about four hours after entering it.

The concentration of Nabatean inscriptions in Wadi Leja is striking. Why did the Nabateans go through this wadi? From its head a path may be followed that leads to the peak of Jebel Musa, but the Nabateans were not Christians and not on a pilgrimage to Jebel Musa. Wadi Leja leads nowhere else. What was the purpose of their travel? The few scattered Nabatean inscriptions in Wadi el-Deir (meaning Wadi of the Monastery, i.e., Saint Catherine's Monastery) and on the saddle of Wadi el-Deir and Wadi Leja do not answer this mystery. So we wondered about the distribution of Nabatean inscriptions. The same phenomenon occurs elsewhere: the Nabateans incised their inscriptions not only along the main roads but also in remote spots.

The Nabateans wrote certain of their graffiti for unclear purposes, perhaps, as students of antiquity tend to say when faced with an inexplicable

---

14. Euting, *Sinaïtische Inschriften*, 9 (inscription 45[a]) and plate 3.

phenomenon, for religious or cultic reasons now unknown. The Nabateans built holy places on mountain peaks such as Jebel Serbal and Jebel Moneijat Musa in Wadi Feiran. Perhaps these inscriptions along cul-de-sacs like Wadi Leja may be explained as being by the way to such mountaintop holy places. Jebel Musa or Jebel Katerina may have been a sacred place for them.

In the afternoon of this day, Tom and I set out to examine Wadi el-Deir. This wadi is an alternative route used by the pilgrims to ascend Jebel Musa. Here, however, in contrast with Wadi Leja, we found no inscriptions of any interest to us. There were some scattered Nabatean inscriptions, although not in the sort of concentration we saw in Wadi Leja, some fairly modern Arabic ones, some crosses incised in the stone, and even a late Russian graffito. No Armenian was to be found. We resurveyed the area on our next visit just to be sure but found nothing more.

As we were walking back, we were suddenly passed by our jeep, with Fathi driving and Uzi as a passenger. Uzi had returned from Feiran and had a most interesting report to make on his mountain climbing. His first impression was of the extraordinary view from the top of the mountain. The climb, he reported, was not excessively hard, although I am sure that those of us less accustomed than he to clambering up these desert peaks would have found it taxing. He had had the fortune to climb up on a night of a full moon; the beauty of its radiance had been astounding. The stars and the moon seem much brighter in the desert than they do in Jerusalem because of the absence of air pollution and because there are no city lights to obscure them.

The Nabateans had a holy place on the peak of Jebel Moneijat Musa, and a number of inscriptions from that site have been published. Uzi discovered twenty-odd inscriptions in the area that had not been recorded by the previous expedition. Some of these were, he assured us, of great interest, including the titles *ikhpala* or *ifkhala* (priest) and *kataba* (scribe). Some were on stones built into the wall by the bedouin custodian, and Uzi either copied them on the spot or prised the stones out and replaced them with others. He located nearly all the inscriptions by the exceptionally bright moonlight and in the morning both copied them carefully and photographed them. Uzi read a number of priestly titles on these inscriptions, a concentration of such titles unparalleled in the entire Nabatean domain. We communicated copies to Avner Goren and to Abraham Negev in Jerusalem, who had published the previous inscriptions from this site.

The bedouin regard this mountain peak as sacred, and bedouin women still visit it on certain nights, together with their flocks of goats, for communion with Musa (i.e., Moses). The present custodian of the site (a particular bedouin who lives in the area and is entrusted with its custody) is, so it seems, a particularly energetic person. The temenos has been restored and the wall about it rebuilt.

It should be remarked that there is a Byzantine monastery on one of the other mountain peaks in this area. Since ancient times Feiran or Pharan has been, after Mount Sinai itself, the most famous site in the Sinai. Traditionally it was identified as the site of the Israelites' battle with the Amalekites; perhaps the Byzantine monastery was built there for that reason.

Above all, however, Uzi was impressed by the sight of the great oasis of Feiran with its thousands of palm trees. This, the largest oasis in the Sinai, was laid out below him and clearly visible in the bright moonlight. He slept on the mountain and descended uneventfully in the morning, succeeded in contacting Fathi and getting a lift, and met our jeep halfway between Saint Catherine's and Feiran. Our investigations, always in search of the Armenians, continually crisscrossed with the paths of the Nabateans, and we were not finished with them yet.

That same evening we set out for the Field School and the Nature Reserves Authority building in Wadi Leja, where Uzi had acquaintances who knew the desert well. We spent quite some time with them gathering information and discussing possible sites of inscriptions. I enquired carefully about other possible sites in the immediate vicinity of Saint Catherine's. It seems that Wadi Leja contains the richest concentration of epigraphic material in the area. Euting recorded the Nabatean inscriptions from Wadi Leja in his 1891 book; I wondered whether he had found them all. The Greek inscriptions from the region near the new chapel and elsewhere along the wadi have not yet been read. Would we find inscriptions farther along Wadi Leja and along the route up the mountain and then down to Saint Catherine's and Wadi el-Deir on the other side? From earliest days, pilgrims commonly followed this way, but we had not yet been able to study it. On our next visit, indeed, we succeeded in penetrating even farther into Wadi Leja and found a little more evidence but nothing dramatic.

Now Tom, Uzi, and I kicked around the ideas we had started to formulate the previous day about the meaning of our finds in western Sinai. One conclusion imposed itself upon us. It arose from the contrast between the route through Wadi Mukattab and that through Wadi Ḥajjaj.

3. THE SECOND EXPEDITION, 9–17 MAY 1979

The few, late Armenian inscriptions from Wadi Mukattab contrasted with the wealth of ancient material from Wadi Ḥajjaj in eastern Sinai. Was the route through eastern Sinai the chief one the Armenians followed, we asked, coming from Jerusalem and the north? This might fit with the geographical facts of the location of Armenia to the northeast of the land of Israel and of Cilician Armenia to the north. Still, the position of the chief centers of Armenian life did not necessarily determine their routes to the south.

We were compelled to conclude that down to the tenth or eleventh century Armenians generally came to the south overland from Jerusalem, through Eilat (Aila) and Wadi Ḥajjaj to Saint Catherine's and Mount Sinai (Jebel Musa). This is, at least, the evidence of the known inscriptions. One question immediately arose in our minds: How did they travel between Wadi Ḥajjaj and Saint Catherine's? The ancient records reckon eight days of travel from Eilat to Mount Sinai, and judging from that, Wadi Ḥajjaj was certainly more than a single day's journey from Jebel Musa. En route between the two, did the travelers overnight and leave more inscriptions? We resolved to examine some of the possible routes the next day to find out.

A different but related matter also arose. An informant at the Field School said that there was a major concentration of inscriptions in western Sinai, at a site called Wadi Abu Natash, which is about a day's camel ride west of Wadi Mukattab. This, combined with the considerations of the preceding paragraph, put Wadi Abu Natash on our agenda. We decided that on our next expedition we would travel west to the sandy plain of the Ramle (sands) and to Wadi Abu Natash. If this turned out to be a rich site with many inscriptions, and if there was no Armenian among the inscriptions there, then in all likelihood Wadi Mukattab and Wadi Feiran never formed part of a significant Armenian pilgrim route. On the next day, on the last morning of this visit, we added one more piece of evidence to support the idea that for Armenians the eastern Sinai route was predominant.

Sunday, 13 May 1979

After the previous day's discussions, we realized that finding Armenian inscriptions was no longer all that mattered. Both their presence or their absence could teach us about the routes of travel. In light of this, Sunday's travel had two goals. First, we would examine certain routes between Wadi Ḥajjaj and Saint Catherine's for inscriptions, in line with our goal of clarifying whether Armenians had come to Jebel Musa via West Sinai. Second, we wished to do further research in the area of Wadi Ḥajjaj, work that had been aborted on the first day of this trip because of the jeep problems. We also wanted to check an inscribed rock in that area that one of the folk at the Field School had mentioned.

We made an early start and first set out to travel one of the routes between Saint Catherine's and Wadi Ḥajjaj. Our working hypothesis was that the people who left so many inscriptions at Wadi Ḥajjaj, and also in Wadi Mukattab and Wadi Leja, must have left some sign, perhaps only scratched crosses but perhaps some inscriptions, to mark their passage between Wadi Ḥajjaj and Mount Sinai. It has often been suggested that the soft sandstone of areas such as Wadi Ḥajjaj and Wadi Mukattab may have encouraged inscriptions. In a complementary way, another theory suggested that the hard granite of other parts of the Sinai might have discouraged ancient graffiti artists. However, the numerous inscriptions we observed on granite rocks in the Sinai—and there must be many more than just those we saw—speak against the view that it was the sandstone of Wadi Ḥajjaj and Wadi Mukattab that was the determining factor. The granite may not have been as attractive to the passing scribbler or scratcher as the softer sandstone, but it was attractive enough to be used. This was particularly so if the granite had developed a dark patina so that a glancing blow would chip away the patina and produce a clear mark.

SINAI SCENES 8
A black-patinaed rock-face drawing board;
men and women, a horse, ibex herds,
an ostrich hunt, a snake, a scorpion,
a gracious she-camel and her foal
cut white into black nigh two millennia ago,
but still bright.
How long to form a patina?

MES

As I grew more experienced, I was able to predict what types of stone face would usually attract inscriptions or drawings. It is true that the inscriptions on granite are sometimes difficult to read because the patina tends

3. THE SECOND EXPEDITION, 9–17 MAY 1979

to flake away and form a wide, shallow marking on the rock. Regardless, geological character alone cannot explain the absence of inscriptions from any given area.

Departing from the administration buildings, we passed the airfield and continued through the Watiyeh Pass and east through Wadi Mara. The Sinai administration had done work toward the paving of a wide road through this wadi, although activity had now stopped there, since the Sinai was to transfer to Egyptian rule in the coming months. The road was a real scar on the impressive landscape, and I readily admit to preferring the rough paths through the wadis to which we had grown accustomed.

We saw few inscriptions of any sort along Wadi Mara. To the right of the road, (i.e., on its south side) we examined two sizeable rocks. The ever-diligent Nabateans had inscribed them, and there were some rock drawings as well. Only a few crosses preserved faint footsteps of some of our pilgrims.

A little farther on, we checked a large sandstone rock of the sort the bedouin call a *hadbe*. We had been told that there were inscriptions on it. We found some Greek inscriptions (one with a Nabatean name in it), some Nabatean inscriptions, and some in Arabic, as well as some rock drawings. This was all that we found in Wadi Mara, and our impression was that this had not been a route of pilgrim travel, although doubtless there had been some traffic through it.

From Wadi Mara we turned into Wadi Arade. We surveyed all the sandstones at the junction of these two wadis carefully, but only a few rock drawings rewarded our efforts. Following up a report of a much-inscribed rock at Jebel Ashka, we attempted to cross from a branch of Wadi Arade into Wadi Ḥajjaj, passing Jebel Ashka on the way. We crossed by a route that was little traveled. Fatḥi had never been to that area, and I wondered whether much vehicular traffic at all had passed that way. With some difficulty, and with Uzi scouting the area ahead on foot, we crossed the sandstone rock saddle into the branch of Wadi Arade. The weather was unusually overcast so that no shadows were seen but nonetheless rather hot, and we felt the heat more as the middle of the day approached. We penetrated a short distance south in this branch of Wadi Ḥajjaj, attempting to find an area that the jeep could navigate. At the same time, we checked all the rocks in the area that we could reach. Our probes to the south proved to be unsuccessful, and no jeep could pass through this branch of the wadi. It will have to be examined by camel or on foot, if at all. In any case, we found some rock drawings in this area, south of Jebel Ashka, a single Nabatean

Fig. 11. The sand dune at Wadi Rum

inscription, and other rock markings, but their meaning was elusive. Frustrated in our attempt to pass through Wadi Ashka to Wadi Ḥajjaj, we retraced our tracks, intending to return through Wadi Arade and to press on to our next target, an area called Wadi Rum.

On the saddle between Wadi Arade and Wadi Rum we ran into some trouble. People had warned us of a great sand dune at the head of Wadi Rum. "But if you succeed in navigating it," they had said, "you will see lots of inscriptions." Indeed, the approach to the saddle leading into Wadi Rum was a hill of fine, white sand—the dune about which we had been cautioned (fig. 11).

As we headed up, the jeep started to lose momentum and finally came to a stop, dug into the sand up to its axles. Uzi's virtuosity now shone. He instructed us to bring stones, which were easy to find in this area abundant with flakes of brittle sandstone. Then we dug around the jeep's sunken wheels, and Uzi jacked the back axle as high as he could using the rather inconvenient jack with which the jeep was equipped. We pushed the stones under the wheels for traction, and Fatḥi drove ahead as far as he could. This method produced an advance of only a meter or two each time, even though the jeep labored and we all pushed as hard as we were able. The moment the jeep wheel moved off the stones, it would sink into the sand. We repeated this procedure until, finally, the right wheels gained purchase on the rock of the saddle, and we were free! Tom was wilting and looked miserable. I put this down to the heat and to our exertions, but I was wrong—as we later discovered.

Once we had made the saddle safely, we turned south in Wadi Arade and headed toward the main east-west road that we had abandoned earlier. We wanted to follow it to the east and then bear north again and explore Wadi Rum, entering it from another point.

About a kilometer and a half west of Wadi Ḥajjaj, we turned off the road to examine a large rock to its north. It bore inscriptions in Nabatean and Arabic and was adorned with some rock drawings. We continued in the direction of Wadi Rum, which indeed runs some way north of the road. We surveyed the sandstone outcroppings between the road and the entrance to Wadi Rum. Like many sandstone areas, the surface was covered with rocks that make a sort of crunching, tinkling sound under the wheels of the jeep. Rock drawings decorated nearly all of the rocks that we examined in this area; we also saw a number of Nabatean inscriptions.

The entrance into Wadi Rum was striking. At a height of some 20 meters above the wadi floor, we looked through a wide niche, almost like a cutting. The way down was easy enough, had we chosen to take it: just a steep slope with no major obstacles visible. The upper part of the slope was stone, or a stony sand, but the lower part of the same fine, white sand that had bogged us down near Jebel Ashka a short time before. We could see the tracks of a jeep down in the wadi and how it had made repeated assaults on the slope of sand before finally succeeding in its ascent. Uzi was quite confident that, if we went down, we would be able to make it up again. Fatḥi, however, was more doubtful and was unwilling to attempt it. Wadi Rum, therefore, in spite of hints of Greek inscriptions implied by its name, which may mean Wadi of the Byzantines or of the Greeks, had to await a future visit.

I think Fatḥi was also concerned about our fuel situation. The jeep was equipped with two fuel tanks, an extra one having been added. One could switch between them with a manual valve. Both had been full when we left in the morning, and together they held 100 liters (26 gallons) of gasoline, more than enough for our needs. However, one of the tanks apparently leaked, for soon after we set out it ran dry, and we had switched to the other. We were worried about running short, a concern not particularly allayed by the fact that the fuel gauge was not working. This was another of those "jeep issues" that hounded us on this trip.

As a result, time was running short because Fathi wanted to get to Bir Sa'al by 4:00 PM. He hoped that he could get some gasoline before the administration point there closed up and went home. Not that there was a fuel station there, but there was an administration vehicle, and they might have been able to let us have a little gasoline. The shortage of fuel was a pity because I had planned to make a systematic, extensive survey of the whole of the Wadi Hajjaj area. We were unable to do that because of the fuel problem, though we did succeed in other aims we had set ourselves.

While surveying all of the rocks in the area we traversed between Wadi Rum and Wadi Hajjaj, we discovered another rock belonging to the Wadi Hajjaj complex of inscribed boulders. The newly identified rock is about 700 meters northwest of Hadbet Hajjaj (Rock I of Negev's reckoning). On it were a number of Nabatean inscriptions as well as handsome petroglyphs. I photographed the inscriptions, and back in Jerusalem I passed them on to Abraham Negev. Later he told me that they were of interest for their extremely brief formulation and for the fact that a number of the names were Safaitic (an old North Arabic dialect) rather than Nabatean. Safaitic was usually written in the South Arabic script, which is the ancestor script of modern (and ancient) Ethiopic. Safaitic names written in Nabatean script hint at the complexity of ancient tribal groups, of trade patterns (the Nabateans were great traders), and of linguistic distribution.

The overcast sky was unfortunate and affected the photographs of the new rock (Rock X, as we dubbed it) as well as the other photographs of inscriptions that we took that day (indeed, it even rained a few drops). The lack of direct sunshine meant that we did not have much contrast or many dark shadows in the photographs, which would have made the epigraphs more legible. The photographs were unsatisfactory and were the only set of pictures taken on all of our missions that disappointed us.

Above I discussed the problems of photography that I faced.[15] Of course, our work was of a quite specific type, attempting to get clear images of inscriptions and rock drawings. Later I regretted not having recorded more of the scenery and the events of this trip. The magnificent color landscape images of the Sinai that Neil Folberg took and published

---

15. See page 24.

3. THE SECOND EXPEDITION, 9–17 MAY 1979

are a great treasure.[16] The history of photography of the Sinai is still to be written, but something may be learned of it in Douglas R. Nickel's book on the mid-nineteenth-century photographer Francis Frith.[17] Much later I was able to consult pictures taken during a 1930 expedition mounted by two Harvard University orientalists, Kirsopp Lake and Robert Blake. As I studied these black and white prints in the basement of the Harvard Semitic Museum, they evoked images of Serabit el-Khadem and the Sinai's brown sandstone cliffs.[18]

I was upset that we did not finish the survey of Wadi Ḥajjaj, but I took some comfort in two considerations. Since I did not finish my work there, I would have to return, as indeed I did. Moreover, Wadi Ḥajjaj was in the part of the Sinai that was to be the last to revert to the Egyptians, so there would still be some weeks in which we could make a return visit. I photographed Rock X, then started my planned survey of Wadi Ḥajjaj. My aim was to examine all of the rocks in this area anew, not only those that we had previously surveyed. We made a start on the southern side of the road and proceeded to reexamine the cliffs and rocks in this area, including Abraham Negev's Rocks I and IV. We viewed the same inscriptions on Rock I that we had previously found, including the large Georgian one and others in Nabatean, Arabic, and Greek. No new Armenian inscriptions were discovered. We also confirmed Negev's characterization of Rock IV as preserving only rock drawings. We visited two large *hadbes* to the southeast of Rock I as well as the sandstone cliffs that run to its east as far as the road. In both of these areas, we observed drawings but no inscriptions.

By now time was short, since it was nearly 3:00 PM. We proceeded directly to Rocks II and III to examine the three inscriptions we had noted the previous Wednesday. I also wished to try to locate certain inscriptions of which Abraham Negev had given me photographs and some others that appeared in his book but that we had not located on our former visit. This unknown material was listed and marked by him as coming from Rock II.

---

16. Neil Folberg, *In a Desert Land: Photographs of Israel, Egypt, and Jordan* (New York: Abbeville, 1998)

17. Douglas R. Nickel, *Francis Frith in Egypt and Palestine: A Victorian Photographer Abroad* (Princeton: Princeton University Press, 2004).

18. For a brief video account of the Lake-Blake expedition, see https://www.youtube.com/watch?v=A4A6fSzhh-E.

We had looked at Rock II on the previous Wednesday with no results. Uzi went off to examine it all over again. He found nothing.

When evaluating the visit to Rock III that I shall describe directly, it should first be remembered that we had devoted the better part of a full working day to this rock on our first trip. We had also spent a couple of hours there the previous Wednesday. On these former visits, we had learned that a rock face that at noon seemed unmarked could be covered with inscriptions visible only in the light of dawn or in the side illumination of the late afternoon. What was unique about this day's weather, as I have already noted, was that clouds covered the sun, diffusing the light, which made it difficult to discern inscriptions.

Much of my time between the first and second visits to the Sinai had been spent poring over the photographs taken, trying to make out the inscriptions. My notebook held a considerable list of queries, points at which I reconstructed a word or a letter. Could I see any of these reconstructions on the rocks? So, one important purpose of my return to Rock III was to verify or disprove these conjectures as much as possible. Sometimes at the particular hour of the day that we were there the rock was more difficult to read than were the photographs, but in a number of cases I was able to verify important conjectures or reconstructions. Reexamination of the actual stone often showed marks or signs that had not been visible on the photographs. It is not surprising that, particularly where the inscription is shallow or erosion has eaten the rock away, a definitive decipherment can be reached only by repeated reading of photographs in conjunction with examinations of the rock itself.

So now, in the course of a short period of time, something like an hour, I discovered another fifteen or so Armenian inscriptions on Rock III! It is impossible to say why they escaped our attention on previous occasions, for I had examined every square centimeter of the rock as closely as possible. But there they were, and among them were the inscriptions that Abraham Negev had photographed but had mistakenly recorded as coming from Rock II. I started, together with Tom, to record, photograph, and measure them and to make preliminary decipherments. I saw that his heart was not in it, or more accurately, his heart was in it, but physically he was feeling terrible. In the end, he just lay down on the ground and said that he felt so ill he could not go on.

I had taken all the photographs, and Uzi was urging me to finish, when I discovered that the film speed setting on the camera was wrong. So I had to make a new set, for I was not sure whether it had been moved by

3. THE SECOND EXPEDITION, 9–17 MAY 1979

accident just then or whether it had been off for some time. Today digital cameras dispel such uncertainties. As I wrote before, that day many of the photographs were not as good as desired. In the end, this was not because of the speed setting but because of the lighting. The inscriptions were plain to the eye, but the absence of shadow made them illegible in photographs.

By the time all this was finished, Tom was feeling even worse. He sat in the front seat of the jeep, and we set out through Wadi Sa'al to Bir Sa'al, where Fathi expected, or at least hoped, to get some gasoline. We arrived there (before 4:00), but the vehicle we had hoped to milk for gasoline had left, so we had to trust to our own supplies. On the way back to the administration buildings at Saint Catherine's, I spent time carefully examining Wadi Sa'al for inscriptions. None was to be seen. Uzi put this down to the fact that this is a dry wadi, with no water source in it; pilgrim caravans probably used other routes.

So, I thought, I should return once more to Wadi Ḥajjaj because it was imperative to finish reexamining the rocks to the north of the road. At that time, I hoped, I would be able to take new photographs of those inscriptions on Rock III that caused us trouble on this cloudy day. Would it be possible to find even more inscriptions in this seemingly inexhaustible repository of Armenian graffiti? Eventually we returned to Wadi Ḥajjaj on our last trip to the Sinai (see fifth expedition below, 124–25).

This was our last evening at Saint Catherine's and we wanted to leave everything in order, just as we had found it. Uzi and I both wrote reports of our discoveries for Avner Goren, and we left him these and the films of the pictures we had taken on his behalf. Tom, as soon as we got in, dropped onto his bed, quite exhausted. He had complained of nausea and discomfort on the way back. Uzi and I put it down to overexertion in the desert heat. All through our travels we were careful to drink large quantities of water in order to avoid dehydration. Despite this, the heat can be exhausting, and we thought that this was what had happened to Tom. I was relieved to see Tom sleep deeply, and, as he awoke during the evening, I made sure that he took something to drink. When we arose in the morning, he seemed much better.

Monday, 14 May 1979

We had decided, this last morning of this trip, to examine Naqb el-Hawa, the Pass of the Winds, on foot. This pass connects the route from the Feiran Oasis in Wadi Sulaf to the valley at the foot of Mounts Catherine and Sinai. The oldest pilgrim texts describe this approach. Through it, for example, Egeria both arrived and departed in the late fourth century, and the pilgrims who came from western Sinai most likely traveled through this route. The area had to be examined by foot, since it is impassable for a vehicle.[19]

Fathi took us as far as he could in the jeep, then we proceeded to the highest point of the pass by foot, without finding any of the inscriptions that we were seeking. When we turned around and looked back, we realized that it was for good reason that the pilgrim descriptions made much of this passage. The view of Jebel Musa, the pilgrims' Mount Sinai, was spectacular. After the pilgrims had toiled through the desert ways of western Sinai and made the steep ascent from Wadi Sulaf, the sight of the mountains must have unfolded before their eyes with dramatic impact.

From the point at which we left the jeep to the high point of the watershed is a walk of about 20 minutes. We had expected to find inscriptions in this segment of the Naqb (pass), but all we found was a single cross and one other unclear sign on a prominent rock to the north of the path. We spread out and searched the rocky area of the watershed on both sides of the path. Two Arabic inscriptions turned up but nothing more.

We pressed on along the path, toward the western end of the Naqb and Wadi Sulaf. As we walked the well-paved path, we considered the psychological factors bearing on the location of graffiti. Perhaps, we surmised, the expectation of the view of Mount Sinai led the pilgrims to press ahead with all possible haste. Thus Felix Fabri in his itinerary (1480–1483) describes the pass itself not at all but waxes poetic on the view of Mount Sinai from there.[20] Here the pilgrims would not linger to leave their names in the rock but hasten toward their goal. Their day's travel must have started early, and it often concluded at Deir el-Arba'in or at Saint Catherine's Monastery, where they spent the night before ascending the holy mountains the next day. Our psychological speculations, of course, were actually attempts after the fact to explain why there were no inscriptions at Naqb el-Hawa.

---

19. Edward H. Palmer described it vividly in *The Desert of the Exodus: Journeys on Foot in the Wilderness of the Forty Years' Wanderings)*, 148–49.

20. See the full translation of his diary in Felix Fabri, *Felix Fabri (Circa 1480–1483 A.D.)*, trans. Aubrey Stewart, 2 vols. in 4 (London: Palestine Pilgrims' Text Society, 1893–1896). See also the lively retelling by H. F. M. Prescott, *Once to Sinai: The Further Pilgrimage of Friar Felix Fabri* (New York: Macmillan, 1958).

3. THE SECOND EXPEDITION, 9–17 MAY 1979

The rocky desert area we were traversing was far from barren, and all sorts of plants grew among the stones covering its surface. One quite large plant had purple, bell-shaped flowers. It was Belladonna, which is also called Deadly Nightshade. There are various explanations of the name Belladonna, which means "beautiful lady." One is that Venetian women used it to dilate their pupils, so as to enhance their beauty. Another relates it to a murderer who poisoned beautiful women with it. Indeed, in large doses it can be fatal, and it was used as a poison in Europe. The bedouin smoke it in small quantities as a remedy for asthma. It is a powerful hallucinogenic, and I was told that some hippies who used it had completely lost their sanity for about two days.

We were not about to experiment with this infamous plant. Instead, having reached the high point of the watershed, we decided to proceed a little farther along the path. In an area of large granite boulders, perhaps 500 meters on, we found a number of Nabatean and Arabic inscriptions and a few Greek letters. I left the path and went along the bed of the wadi for some distance, for often the path is on the southern side, above the wadi bed for fear of flash flooding.[21] There I discovered a few more Arabic inscriptions. While I was searching these areas, Uzi proceeded briskly along the path. The boulders I mentioned petered out, and then, after about another kilometer, they resumed. In that area he found numerous Nabatean and some Arabic inscriptions.

At this point we turned back. Time was pressing, and we had our arrangements to make before departing for the airfield, which we had set for noon. Fathi was to pick us up at 10:30. On our way out we found one more cross and the Greek letters XC, that is, "Christos," and a single Nabatean inscription on the eastern side of the watershed.

The results of our probe seemed clear enough. On this last stage of their odyssey, the pilgrims from the west were too excited at the prospect of its impending climax to spend time incising their names on the abundant granite rocks. Yet it seemed likely that they had left inscriptions, so we surmised, at their last stopping place before Naqb el-Hawa, which was most probably at an oasis called Sheikh 'Awad or one of the other water sources some distance farther to the west than we had penetrated. We regretted that, on Saturday, when we followed the path of Wadi Sulaf,

---

21. Palmer quotes a striking description of one of these flash floods: "a boiling, roaring torrent filled the entire valley, carrying down huge boulders of rock as though they had been so many pebbles" (*Desert of the Exodus*, 151–52).

we had not continued as far as was possible in an easterly direction. Perhaps, we hoped, we would be able to make that trip on another occasion and cover the short distance between our easternmost and westernmost penetrations of this area.

Of course, our speculations about the pilgrims' motivations and concerns were just that—speculations. One can gain some insight into a pilgrim's state of mind from rather personal narratives like that of the fifteenth-century German monk Felix Fabri. Many pilgrim reports, however, lack Fabri's autobiographical and narrative bent, only briefly mentioning the holy places visited or the holy or ascetic men and women seen; the amount of circumstantial "color" is limited. However, we did make a not altogether vain attempt to predict where we might search with a reasonable chance of finding inscriptions.

Since we exited from the Naqb some time before the hour appointed for our meeting with Fathi, we decided to examine Wadi Tlah, which is abundantly endowed with water. The bedouin carry on extensive agricultural activity there and have gardens and orchards surrounded by carefully tended stone walls. The plastic pipes commonly used in the modern agricultural operations in Israel supply the fields with water. Alongside them the old counterweighted poles with buckets that were previously used for irrigation still stand by idly.

Perhaps the most picturesque and beautiful [wadi] ... is the Wády T'láh, ... a fertile and well-watered glen, which one would little expect to find in the midst of such utter desolation. Between steep and fantastic rocks you look down a long vista of verdant gardens, and listen to the grateful sound of a brawling stream that dashes along past thickets of fruit-trees, and falls ever and anon over smooth fern-clad boulders.[22]

We entered the wadi to the west of the walled gardens. By then Tom was feeling ill again, so I decided to go slowly with him while Uzi advanced quickly so he could come out at the other end of the wadi. He left at a brisk pace, while we started to descend slowly. We examined the bedouin gardens, then started to clamber down the rocks into the wadi. They were several meters high and formed quite a steep descent. The ground was damp, and at some spots there were pools of water. Green plants grew, and the whole was rather luxuriant. We did not enjoy much of it, however, for Tom's illness turned out to be a type of dysentery. I feared he would have

---

22. So Palmer describes this spot in *Desert of the Exodus*, 124.

difficulty climbing back out of the wadi, but my fears were dispelled. We ascended slowly, with Tom taking rests at each stage. Finally we worked our way up to the rendezvous point, still far too early. I got Tom to lie in the shade of a rock and waited impatiently for Fathi. He was there on time. In short order, we were back at Saint Catherine's and consulted the doctor at the excellent clinic there. He diagnosed Tom's complaint and prescribed some medicine and continual drinking, for he was also suffering from dehydration.

The flight back to Jerusalem was uneventful by comparison with our vicissitudes in Wadi Tlah. We had an hour stopover in Eilat. Tom spent it lying on a bench sipping from a glass of water. He was sick all the way back to Jerusalem, and by the time we arrived he was a little delirious. He was indisposed for several more days, which he spent in the spare room at my house, and we took good care of him.

Uzi and I were also afflicted in greater or lesser measure by the same illness a day or two later; we never discovered what particular cause was to blame. Looking back, I recalled that Fathi also had been feeling unwell the second day we were in Wadi Mukattab. Being a bedouin, he did not do anything about it and let it interfere as little as possible with our work.

The results of this expedition, then, provided the beginning of our theories about the chief pilgrim routes in the Sinai, particularly those of the Armenian pilgrims. The absence of inscriptions is not an infallible sign, but their presence is highly significant. It was hard to avoid weighing against one another the fifty-odd early Armenian inscriptions from the single site of Wadi Hajjaj and the thin finds in the extensively inscribed Wadi Mukattab. We decided on our next steps after considering the implications of this comparison. We would examine the passes over the Tih, the mountain massif in western Sinai, particularly the important pass called Naqb Rakna. After that we would further investigate western Sinai, particularly Wadi Abu Natash, where we had heard rumor of a remarkable concentration of inscriptions. Finally, we would explore the routes between Eilat (Aila), Wadi Hajjaj, and the Saint Catherine's area in greater detail.

4
The Third Expedition: The Central Sinai Route
16–18 June 1979

Saturday, 16 June 1979

Preparations for the third expedition to the Sinai, exactly one month after our return, were rather hasty. The impending reversion of western Sinai to Egypt infused us all with a sense of urgency. Would the Egyptians let us go on with our work? They had promised to let research continue, but what would they actually do when they gained control? In the event, our sense of urgency proved completely justified. The Egyptians did not want Israelis moving off the paved roads in the Sinai and wandering around the desert; indeed, Israeli research there came to an end after the Sinai finally reverted to Egyptian rule.

At this pressing juncture I was more than grateful for the support of Provost Vartan Gregorian of the University of Pennsylvania. Vartan had taken an interest in the Sinai work from its inception, and his support was invaluable. As a result, I had a modest sum of money at my disposal that made this expedition possible.

My aim was to check out my hypotheses about the pilgrims, their routes, and the distribution of graffiti, as well as to follow up on some information I had received about inscriptions. The early pilgrim reports speak mostly of travel through western Sinai. However, in contrast to the pilgrim itineraries, our finds indicated that, if the frequency of the occurrence of inscriptions is an indicator, it was unusual for Armenians to travel that way.

My theory was that Armenian pilgrim traffic to Mount Sinai came predominantly through eastern Sinai rather than via the western route. We had studied Wadi Maghara, Wadi Feiran, Wadi Mukattab, and Wadi el-Sheikh. These wadis combine to constitute the desert highway leading to Mount Sinai from the west. The evidence there for Armenian travelers was pitifully thin and late. We planned to check a reported concentration of inscriptions at Wadi Abu Natash, a day's travel southwest of Wadi Mukattab. If that was a major site and if its contents resembled those of Wadi Mukattab (i.e., if it had many inscriptions but few Armenian), that would confirm our tentative view that Armenian pilgrim traffic through western Sinai was sparse. Other non-Armenian pilgrims and travelers wrote numerous graffiti in Wadi Mukattab, so it is reasonable to infer that, if the western Sinai was a major Armenian route, more than the few scattered Armenian graffiti that we found would have been written.

Another possible eastern approach to Mount Sinai was from a Negev town such as Nessana or Gaza from the northeast, approaching Mount Sinai by traveling southward across the Tih, the wasteland plateau of central Sinai. After descending from the Tih, the pilgrims still had to traverse some wadis in western Sinai in order to reach Mount Sinai, traveling southwest. To check whether Armenians used this route, I wished to examine Naqb Rakna, in western Sinai. This is the most important of the passes descending from the Tih, northeast of Saint Catherine's. If we found significant Armenian inscriptions in that area, I would need to revise my western Sinai hypothesis.

Given the transfer of authority, the trip was urgent, but it proved difficult to arrange at short notice for the same reason. Avner, the chief archaeologist, and his staff were fully occupied by the withdrawal from western Sinai. They had to ferry all their gear back to Israel and to finish up whatever of their own projects they could before the withdrawal. They were in the field all the time. Eventually I did succeed in contacting them, but they told me that their one jeep was busy until after the withdrawal.

I was in some despair, but the thought of what we might miss stiffened my resolve and stimulated me into one last attempt. I finally got hold of Benny and asked: Could we go down to Saint Catherine's and rent a jeep there from one of the bedouin? Yes, Benny would arrange that, and Avner and he would give us all necessary assistance.

The chances of our being allowed to carry out this work after the Egyptians assumed control of western Sinai were uncertain; as already noted, later on our doubts were confirmed: the Egyptians did not want Israeli researchers driving freely around the desert. Uzi strongly encouraged me—and his urgings were very much to the point. After our joint trip, which is the subject of the present chapter, he not only mounted a brief expedition to Mount Serbal near Wadi Feiran, where he investigated an important Nabatean sanctuary on its peak, but also rented a small plane

4. THE THIRD EXPEDITION, 16–18 JUNE 1979

and examined many of the high peaks in the Sinai, noting the existence of Nabatean sanctuaries on them.

This was still in the future, however, when I boarded the plane at Ben Gurion Airport early on the morning of Saturday, 16 June 1979. The airport had a deserted, closed feeling to it. It was the Sabbath, and there was no flight from Jerusalem. This time I left Jerusalem on my own; Tom was touring the country with his brother and unable to join me on this trip. Uzi, however, boarded the plane in Eilat and spent the three days of this expedition with me.

The view of the Sinai on the way down from Eilat to Saint Catherine's was exceptionally fine. We flew down parallel to the Sinai coast, and the coral formations in the coastal waters were clearly visible from the air. Then, at a point past Nweiba, the airplane turned inland and headed toward the Mount Sinai airfield, about 20 kilometers from Saint Catherine's and Jebel Musa, which were already familiar from our previous journey. Below and to the north of the plane we could see Wadi Zalaqa. This long wadi cuts south-southwest from near Eilat to debouch some distance north of the Saint Catherine's area. We had received reports of some "Armenian" inscriptions in this area, and it became the goal of one of our later expeditions.

The airplane landed at the Mount Sinai airport at 9:30, and Shauly, Avner Goren's assistant, met us together with the promised jeep, which he had fueled and provisioned. With the jeep came a driver, a bedouin named Ḥmed of the Jebaliyeh bedouin tribe that lives near Saint Catherine's. He was a careful driver, perhaps even too slow; the jeep was his responsibility, however, and we could not criticize him. We had to secure permits to pass through the new army check post in Wadi Feiran. The Feiran check post, still the bedouin center, became the Israeli-Egyptian border crossing for some months shortly afterward.

Past the check post, we bore roughly north for about 30 kilometers on a road that ran into Wadi Aḥdar. We stopped at the oasis called 'Ein Aḥdar (i.e., the Aḥdar Spring) in this wadi (fig. 12). The Arabic word *'ein* and its Hebrew cognate *'ayin* both mean "spring," and both also mean "eye." Oddly, the Armenian word *akn* also means both "spring" and "eye." Arabic and Hebrew are both Semitic languages, while Armenian belongs to the large Indo-European group of languages. This is a striking coincidence in meanings between languages that have no genetic relationship.

There were many bedouin at the spring watering their camels and performing other domestic chores. Walled areas enclosed green groves of trees and gardens, as is the usual practice in bedouin agriculture. We had

Fig. 12. At 'Ein Aḥdar

observed the same sort of walled gardens in Wadi Leja, between Jebel Musa and Jebel Katerina, and also in Wadi Tlaḥ. In Wadi Aḥdar, just past the point where all the camels and bedouin were milling around, quite close to us, we saw an Egyptian vulture. Like all members of its family, it is a large bird but has distinctive light underfeathers and black feathers on the wings and tail. We had seen another in Wadi Ḥajjaj at the beginning of our adventures. In general, birds abounded along this route. The wadi itself is in the red granite country typical of this central area of southern Sinai.

In the distance we could see the cliffs of the Tih, the mountainous plateau of central Sinai. We hoped that study of the passes descending from the Tih would provide some indication about Armenian traffic along the central Sinai route. Our immediate destination was Naqb Rakna, one of the chief passes by which travelers can descend from the Tih plateau into southern Sinai.

To reach Naqb Rakna from 'Ein Aḥdar, we drove southwest along the course of Wadi Aḥdar for about another 20 kilometers. Then we reached Wadi Labwa (Wadi of the Lions). This wadi was part of a frequently used route that runs from Tih and Naqb Rakna at one end to the Saint Catherine's Monastery area at the other. For that reason, as we passed by we

4. THE THIRD EXPEDITION, 16–18 JUNE 1979

Map 4. From Naqb Rakne to Wadi Abu Natash

examined the rocky sides of the wadi carefully for inscriptions. A little over five kilometers into the wadi, we saw a large rock standing in a prominent position on the southwestern side of the valley, The name of this rock is Hajar el-La'awa, and it is a well-known site. This was exactly the sort of rock that, in our experience, attracted the attention of ancient writers of graffiti who liked to write on a prominent place. When we examined it, we saw that it was indeed covered with writing; a large number of Nabatean inscriptions, one in Latin letters saying "AK 1858," some graffiti in Arabic, and some crosses. Behind it was a fairly smooth rock face that had also attracted the attention of the ancient graffiti writers. I could imagine a traveler stopping, perhaps for a brief rest, at Hajar el- La'awa and writing on this prominent rock or wandering behind it and being attracted by the smooth rock face.

We photographed Hajar el- La'awa as well as the inscriptions we discovered on the rock face behind it. Traveling further along Wadi Labwa, we passed by another water source, Bir Miserih, a short distance from the track, and some time later we turned northeast and reached the large oasis of Bir Iqna.

There was no one at this oasis, even though a number of bedouin dwellings stood there, and there were extensive agricultural gardens of the sort we had seen before, as well as two monuments. Called *sheikhs*, these are tombs of notable tribal leaders; they are usually low buildings with a domed roof. One of these is called Sheikh Ghanm, and the other is the tomb of a woman leader, Omariyah. She had led the tribes of western Sinai in a war against those of eastern Sinai, an event that took place, I was informed, about three centuries ago. Our driver, Ḥmed, however, had never heard of this great event. At Bir Iqna there was particularly luxuriant growth of the Arabian rush (*Juncus arabicus*, which is the Hebrew *semar 'aravi*). It grows in clumps and is used in the weaving of matting. According to some authorities, it may have also served in former times to make styluses for writing, by cutting the stem at an angle. We also saw another Egyptian vulture there as well as a pair of ravens. In Sinai, wherever there is water, there is life! Here was life indeed ... but no inscriptions. As I have already remarked, for whatever reason inscriptions are rare at water sources.

We returned to Wadi Labwa from Bir Iqna, a distance of just over 3 kilometers, and proceeded along this wadi until it ran into Wadi 'Ajar. After a short time continually bearing northwest, we crossed the rocky saddle at the end of Wadi 'Ajar and traversed a tortuous, stony valley of red granite (Wadi Bireq). The rocky terrain threw our jeep and its passengers around mercilessly. On the way, there were particularly large flocks of sheep and goats at pasture; we also saw a black kite (*Milvus migrans,* a bird of prey) perched on a rock not 50 meters from the jeep. It flew off as we approached.

At 1:15 PM we reached Wadi Siḥ, a flat, sandy valley that was a pleasant contrast to the rough ride we had suffered in Wadi Bireq. About ten

4. THE THIRD EXPEDITION, 16–18 JUNE 1979

Fig. 13. The Tih and Naqb Rakna

minutes after entering Wadi Siḥ, we passed Sheikh Ḥmed, a stone structure with a tin roof and graves clustered around it. We did not enter the wadi at its head but about halfway along its length, where Wadi Bireq ran into it. The territory flattened out and became increasingly sandy, with a reddish tint to the sand. By the time we reached the end of Wadi Siḥ, there was before us a great, sandy plain dotted with green plants. This was sandstone country, and there were large outcroppings of sandstone scattered throughout. This sandy area is known as "the sands," *ramleh* in Arabic. The word is also the name of the city in central Israel called Ramleh (Hebrew Ramlah).[1]

Our plan was to survey as many of the sandstone outcroppings as we could, working our way gradually toward the bottom of the Tih at the point at which Naqb Rakna debouches into the sands.

The descent from the plateau of the Tih through the Naqb Rakna pass is perilous (fig. 13). Felix Fabri describes it, and a mishap that befell his

---

1. The city of Ramleh was founded circa 705–715 CE by the Umayyad Caliph Suleiman ibn Abed al-Malik after the Arab conquest of the region. It is the only old city in Israel founded by the Arab invaders.

group of pilgrims while they were making their way down. Their descent took nearly five hours. In the course of it, a number of camels fell, including that which contained the groups' medicine chest. Felix Fabri remarks that one of his companions made his journey in a pannier on the camel's back, and fortunately he was persuaded to alight and descend by foot, else he might have suffered the fate of the medicine chest.[2]

We headed for a large rock in the area close to the exit from Wadi Siḥ. After finding Nabatean drawings and inscriptions, we enjoyed lunch in a small patch of shade formed by its western corner. The sun was still in the east, and on the rock's east side were more rock drawings. Ahead, to the right and at some distance, we could see the long escarpment of the Tih, separated from us by a wide plain of yellow sand. In contrast, to our left and over against the Tih we could see black mountains, including Serabit el-Khadem, the famous site of turquoise mines that were exploited by the Egyptians as early as the third millennium BCE.[3]

Coming to Mount Sinai via this central route involved traveling south from a site in the Negev and a long journey over barren ground covered with white dust. One staging point in the Negev for pilgrims was the Nabatean town of Nessana (Nitsana), where sixth- and seventh-century papyri in Greek and Arabic have been discovered. These provide a good deal of information about daily life in a Nabatean city at that time. One papyrus (P. Colt 89) records that a group of traders paid an Arab escort to take them to the holy mountain, showing how enterprising bedouin (called Saracens in many ancient sources) made a good living serving the pilgrims' needs.[4]

We proceeded about 4 kilometers to the east and examined the western approaches to Jebel Ḥemiyar, a large rocky area from which the sands took their full name, Ramlet Ḥemiyar, the Sands of Ḥemiyar. We could not examine the whole of this great mass of sandstone rock due to lack of time but checked selected spots of its western side, with no results at all. On a flat face of stone at the southern end of a small rock with a dark patina,

---

2. H. F. M. Prescott, *Once to Sinai: The Further Pilgrimage of Friar Felix Fabri* (New York: Macmillan, 1958), 70.

3. See pages 85–86 below.

4. Casper J. Kraemer Jr., *Excavations at Nessana III: Non-literary Papyri* (Princeton: Princeton University Press, 1958), nos. 72 and 73; and Philip Mayerson, "The Pilgrim Routes to Mount Sinai and the Armenians," *Israel Exploration Journal* 32 (1982): 44–57.

4. THE THIRD EXPEDITION, 16–18 JUNE 1979

we did discover an extraordinary number of Nabatean inscriptions. This rock face, roughly triangular in shape, is just northeast of Jebel Ḥemiyar.[5] The eastern side of the same rock bore further Nabatean inscriptions and a single cross.[6] The numerous Nabatean inscriptions on this rock stimulated us to search others in the same area. We did so, but with no success.

We then worked our way from the area of Jebel Ḥemiyar toward the mouth of Naqb Rakna, carefully examining all the rocks in a broad area in this direction. The terrain changed as we approached Naqb Rakna, although we were still a few kilometers from the foot of the Tih. It became increasingly stony, with many larger and smaller pieces of stone lying on the surface Watercourses had worked their way into the ground, producing small gulches that were difficult to traverse with the jeep. Uzi was driving and getting everything he could out of the vehicle. Ḥmed had lain down to rest in the back, but as Uzi's driving became more and more adventuresome, he sat up and watched him in increasing tension. Uzi, as I already noted, was an excellent driver and would broach obstacles that frightened lesser drivers. I must confess that I was sometimes tense when he was particularly daring, but my faith in his ability never wavered.

The plain, sandy at first but increasingly rocky, is 600–700 meters above sea level, while the very top of the Tih in this area is about 1,100 meters. So Naqb Rakna was roughly a half kilometer drop. As we approached it in the bouncing jeep, the two sides of the Naqb (i.e., the pass) could easily be seen.

In the end, Ḥmed's concern for the safety of the jeep overcame other considerations, and we abandoned it about 2.5 kilometers from the base of Naqb Rakna. Ḥmed remained with the vehicle, but Uzi and I decided to proceed on foot to the base of the defile, to see whether the great stone faces at that point held any inscriptions. The approaches to the foot of the Naqb were seemingly level ground covered with scattered stones. In fact, shallower and deeper ravines traversed this terrain. The going was quite hard, particularly at the end of a long day; by now, it was about 5:00 in the afternoon, and I had left home eleven hours earlier, at 6:00 that morning.

Throughout this rocky area were clear signs of human activity: stone structures that had collapsed into heaps of rock, perhaps half a meter high and a meter long, and some large stone-walled enclosures whose purpose was unclear—they did not seem to be temenoi, or sacred precincts.

---

5. Rock Inscriptions Project sites 84 and 85. See http://rockinscriptions.huji.ac.il/inscriptionSite/index.

6. Rock Inscriptions Project sites 82 and 83.

Stone heaps and cairns abounded, which were result of human activity that, Uzi informed us, dated from the third or fourth millennium BCE. Their function was not evident, but Uzi surmised that they had served as wind breaks for people sleeping after the descent from the Tih or before making the ascent. We were about to discover the plain's prevailing winds for ourselves that night. Nonetheless, we wondered who could have slept on that stony ground, for no attempt seemed to have been made to clear the ground behind the windbreaks. Uzi went on as far as the actual rock face at the base of the Naqb. It was completely free of inscriptions, but, of course, it was late and impossible to tell whether our survey had exhausted the possibilities of that area. Indeed, later conversations with people who had spent time in the area of Naqb Rakna indicated that there might be inscriptions there.

SINAI SCENES 9
Ancient sanctuaries with standing stones,
a temple on a mountaintop,
cells, monasteries, and holy sites;
Black, chipped flint knives,
cairns, crenellations, roads, and paths,
round postbox tombs,
beehives built of dry rock,
dotting the sand.

MES

It was twilight when we reached the jeep and set off for Wadi Abu Natash. We entered Wadi Siḥ, the route we had to follow to reach our next destination, but did not get far, for we carefully checked all the rocky outcroppings on the way. We were in the process of examining a large rocky mass called Umm Araq, crowned at its northern end by a massive tiered hill of sandstone, when darkness fell. Before it was completely dark, we managed to make out numerous Nabatean drawings and inscriptions and at least one South Arabic inscription.

In darkness, we drove a distance of about 2 kilometers in search of a location free of the prevailing wind that penetrated every corner and crevice. The landscape was still more or less pure quartz sand, very fine, of the sort that is lovely for children to have in their sandboxes. Where it was banked up against rocks, the sand had a rippled surface, rather like waves.[7]

That night we slept by the jeep under the open sky, after a pleasant meal and the tea without which the bedouin find it hard to eat, or even to pass the day. Tea, and not coffee, is an everyday drink, sugary and sometimes flavored by a rose bud.

Sunday, 17 June 1979

We rose rather early, at least Uzi and I did, at about 4:30 AM, and in the desert that dawn hour was lovely. Ḥmed, much more accustomed than I to sleeping out in the desert, managed to sleep until we had finished fueling the jeep, repacking it, having breakfast, and generally readying ourselves for the day's work. From tracks in the sand, we discovered that there had been a nocturnal visitor, a fox, but it certainly did not disturb our gear or us. The sandy desert area has quite a lot of wildlife, and in the sand by where we had camped the distinctive imprints of lizards abounded— a single line drawn by the tail and small footprints on either side of it. Indeed, we spotted an exceptionally large lizard, a Sinai agama (*Pseudotrapelus sinaitus*; formerly *Agama sinaita*; in Hebrew *hardon sinai*), which has a striking blue head and neck and grows up to about 25 centimeters long (9.8 inches).[8] The bedouin trap and eat them, as they are considered a delicacy. We also saw some birds and many bird tracks in the sand. Later, on our way back in the dark from Wadi Abu Natash to Saint Catherine's, we also sighted a hare that ran across the road ahead of us.

On this day, we aimed first to complete the work we had started at Umm Araq near our overnight stop.[9] Then we planned to leave the area of the sands and to proceed to Wadi Abu Natash by way of a series of wadis that bore first southwest and then northwest, always moving farther from Saint Catherine's.

---

7. Wilfred Thesiger, *Arabian Sands* (New York: Dutton, 1959), pl. 4; see also 119–20, where he discusses various configurations of rippling sand.

8. For remarkable pictures of this blue lizard, see https://en.wikipedia.org/wiki/Sinai_agama.

9. Umm ʿAraq (Rock Inscription Project site 87) occurs on the maps as elevation point 713, and its coordinates are 4578 2174 UTM. This rock must be distinguished from the site called Jebel Umm ʿAraq in southern Sinai.

We retraced the drive from our camping site to Umm ʿAraq. This rocky mass is several kilometers in circumference. We started to work our way around it, commencing at the eastern side. Immediately we came upon a group of rock drawings and inscriptions. Nearly all the inscriptions we found on the eastern side, and indeed almost everywhere on this rock, were in Nabatean. In the last light of the previous day it had seemed to us that we saw crosses on Umm ʿAraq, and by the morning sunlight we discovered a few more. Not a single letter in Greek turned up, nor any in Armenian. Even Arabic inscriptions were rare.

On the northeast corner of Umm ʿAraq we spied a flat rock face with a dark patina absolutely covered with Nabatean inscriptions. At its foot lay a large rock on which were yet more, and a further group occurred in the next niche around. We photographed them all. We discovered a further concentration of inscriptions at the southwest corner of this rock; again, Nabatean inscriptions predominated, but there were some rock drawings and a South Arabic inscription that we transcribed. On its south side is a square stone bedouin building, close by which is a bedouin cemetery. Upon our return to Jerusalem I gave photographs of this material to the epigrapher Joseph Naveh, who has since passed away, but no distinct publication of this remarkable find has appeared.

Umm ʿAraq was a fitting conclusion to our visit to the area of the sands and Naqb Rakna. We completed our survey of this remarkable site by 7:15 AM and set off for Wadi Abu Natash. We had surveyed a number of the rocks that dot the sandy plain, extending 10 or so kilometers from the foot of the Tih. We had made a more cursory examination of the rocky area at the foot of the Tih itself, made of boulders washed down from the escarpment. The sand extends quite a way farther south than the edge of the plain, and I have already remarked that the bed of Wadi Siḥ is partly covered with this same sort of white sand. What was of interest was that, even though our examination of the areas close by the foot of the Tih was not exhaustive, we had checked most of the prominent rocks and mountains between the end of the Naqb Rakna Pass and the entry into Wadi Siḥ. [10] Topography requires that this be the chief route travelers follow between Naqb Rakna and Saint Catherine's. Of these rocks, many were innocent of any writing, and on the others the only signs of Christian travelers were a few crosses. However, we know from

---

10. Rock Inscriptions Project site 80.

travelers' reports that this was one of the pilgrim routes, though not a very major one.

For this reason, the meager results of our survey of Wadi Rakna area do not prove that there was no Christian pilgrimage by that route. Had the political circumstances of the day been different, we should have made a far more detailed survey of all the passes down from the Tih into South Sinai. In spite of this lacuna, imposed by circumstances, it is surely significant that, among the numerous inscriptions we discovered, only a few crosses witnessed to the passage of Christians.

We were particularly excited about the site named Wadi Abu Natash. As mentioned, we had it from reliable sources that a major group of inscriptions was there. Apart from the fact that it was important in its own right, the presence or absence of Armenian inscriptions would have direct bearing on our views about the routes of Armenian pilgrims. To judge from the map, it seemed likely that, on the route from the Gulf of Suez to Saint Catherine's, Wadi Abu Natash was the last way station before Wadi Mukattab.

Wadi Siḥ afforded easy passage, and we followed it as far as the area where it runs into Wadi Sidri. This was beyond the point at which we had entered Wadi Sidri the previous day. On both sides granite mountains, with pink or red color predominating, bounded the part of Wadi Sidri along which we now traveled. It seemed to be quite forbidding, and although we kept a sharp watch, we found no inscriptions of any sort in this stretch of about 25 kilometers. Wadi Sidri runs into Wadi Mukattab, which is actually topographically part of it, and resumes after Wadi Mukattab ends. Wadi Mukattab was a familiar sight for us, for on our previous visit (the second expedition) we had spent a lot of time walking its length. This time we passed through quickly, entering at 8:30 AM and not pausing to renew our acquaintance with the inscriptions at this remarkable site. Our minds were set on Wadi Abu Natash and the riches we hoped to find there.

After the end of Wadi Mukattab, the valley broadens notably as the traveler reenters Wadi Sidri. The entrance to Wadi Maghara is off this track just before Sheikh Suleiman Nafa'i (Nafa'i is the name of one of the bedouin tribes), a tomb holy to the bedouin by which is a well. We passed it, and then, shortly after, on the northern side of the wadi, we spotted a rock with inscriptions. They were Nabatean and modern English, and we also found a cross. At 9:00 we entered Wadi Budra, having voyaged 47 kilometers from Umm 'Araq. This section of the journey was over terrain that was difficult in parts, with the road making many steep descents. The geological makeup of this region was notable. Great forces have caused a displacement of the strata so that all the rocky prominences exhibit strata lying at an angle of about 30 degrees to level ground. This part of the Sinai is typified by striking varicolored sand, with swaths of the colors red, yellow, and purple. The result is quite extraordinary. These colors result from the oxidation of minerals prevalent in this area, particularly iron and manganese. After traveling about 8 kilometers through Wadi Budra, we turned onto a paved road that the Egyptians had built. They had maintained mines not far from there from which they had extracted manganese, kaolin, and sand used for glass manufacture. In this, they followed the practice of the British. As we traveled along this road, we noted two or three sites containing drawings and inscriptions that I shall describe shortly.

The road had inadequate storm water drainage, particularly where it crossed Wadi Shellaleh. As a consequence, it had washed away in some of the flash floods, but the lively traffic along these ways had created small detours that were passable; we used them to pick our rather makeshift way around the washouts. After 3 kilometers or so we came to an area where the black of manganese could be seen as it spilled down the mountainside; the manganese mines were visible in the mountainside. This explained the curious epiphany of an ore cart I had observed some kilometers before, along the road through Wadi Budra. At 9:27 AM we entered Wadi Abu Natash.

Here we experienced a considerable disappointment. At the start of the wadi was a bedouin encampment consisting chiefly of corrugated iron shanties. We passed through this and into the wadi. It was not very wide, and we soon came to a spot where we could not pass easily. Stones blocked part of the road, and the rest passed under an acacia tree. This tree, one of several varieties that grow throughout the Sinai, has long, hard thorns (fig. 14). Camels and goats eat its lower branches, and its thorns carpet the ground beneath the tree and are a sure promise of puncture if one drives under it. We decided to clear the ground under one tree by hand and passed successfully. Soon, however, we came to another. Uzi and Ḥmed went ahead to scout the wadi, for as far as we had gone we had found no signs of inscriptions. There were many drawings, often unusual, with numerous fertility symbols. Rocks and acacias effectively blocked the way, and it seemed unlikely that we would find any inscriptions there.[11]

---

11. The acacia is thought to be the wood of which Exodus says the ark of the

4. THE THIRD EXPEDITION, 16–18 JUNE 1979

Fig. 14. An acacia in the Sinai

Mining has disfigured the natural beauty of Wadi Abu Natash. Unsightly gray tailings from the kaolin mines have poured down the side of the mountains. Moreover, it became evident to us that this was a dry wadi, with no source of water in it. Our growing disappointment was compounded when we also managed to get a flat tire despite our careful removal of all the thorns. So we gave up and left the wadi, having penetrated about a kilometer by jeep and another kilometer or so on foot. We stopped at the bedouin encampment to make enquiries, and here Muhammad, who was about ten years old, adopted us. He explained that there were no inscriptions in Wadi Abu Natash but that there were some in the immediately adjoining Wadi Shellaleh.[12] He guided us to a site some meters farther along the road than the entrance to Wadi Abu Natash. This

---

covenant was built (called šiṭṭah in Hebrew, seyyal in Arabic). See Exod 25:10, 13: They shall make an ark of acacia wood; it shall be two and a half cubits long, a cubit and a half wide, and a cubit and a half high. ... You shall make poles of acacia wood, and overlay them with gold." Compare also Isa 41:19: "I will put in the wilderness the cedar, the acacia, the myrtle, and the olive; I will set in the desert the cypress, the plane and the pine together" (NRSV). In the latter text, only the acacia is a true desert tree, and that is why this hopeful prophecy is striking. The name *acacia* actually designates a large family of plants, most varieties of which are in Australia, and most of the acacias outside Australia have thorns. This tree is a common sight in the Sinai and also in the Negev and Judean Deserts.

12. Rock Inscriptions Project sites 90–97.

was part of Wadi Shellaleh. On a large, flat rock at the north side of the road we discovered about fifteen Greek inscriptions, some crosses, and some Nabatean inscriptions. A few more turned up on rocks elsewhere in this same part of the wadi. There are several sites bearing the name Shellaleh, which means "waterfall."

While we were busy examining this find, making notes, and photographing, Ḥmed took the jeep to the bedouin garage on the other side of the road. After we finished work, we joined him. About half a dozen men were sitting in a small shelter built of stone. One had a stripped-down truck motor in front of him on the ground, placed on a piece of old carpet. He had disassembled it completely, and the cam, clean and greased, was beside him (he was overhauling the engine). There was no workbench, only a few tools around, and he was cleaning parts of the motor as he squatted on his haunches. These men gave us water, then tea, and we had quite a long conversation with them. Among other things, they told us that there used to be inscriptions on the rocks in Wadi Abu Natash but that the British and the Egyptians had destroyed them in the course of mining and road building. Muhammad indicated to us that he had more to show us, so we took leave of the garage and headed back down the road.

On our way to Wadi Abu Natash on the paved road, we had observed a number of large fallen rocks with rock drawings a kilometer or somewhat less before the entrance to it. That part of the road follows Wadi Shellaleh. The rocks contained many Nabatean inscriptions and a great number of rock drawings. After we spent time there, Muhammad told us that we should proceed even farther down to the road. We came to a point at which the road takes a hairpin bend, fairly high on the side of the wadi. Here we left the jeep and climbed down onto the wadi floor. First we came to a large rock with an overhang above us. It had Greek inscriptions in quite large numbers and many Nabatean inscriptions all over the accessible part. There were numerous rock drawings, including a particularly finely done pair of Egyptian boats. A drawing of a man on a horse, perhaps one of the equestrian saints, surmounted a long, two-line Greek inscription.[13]

A hundred meters farther down the wadi we observed another rock covered with numerous Nabatean inscriptions, and behind it yet another, with more Nabatean. The first of these two was notable for the fact that the floods had apparently washed away the ground under one end, so it

---

13. Compare Rock Inscriptions Project 2081.

was tilted with the inscriptions at an angle along its face. Still farther down the wadi we found more rocks with Nabatean inscriptions and some rock drawings, but no Greek and no crosses.[14]

The number of inscriptions here was large, a concentration second only to Wadi Mukattab among the sites we had seen. The relatively small number of Greek inscriptions was the same phenomenon that we had previously observed. We found no Armenian inscriptions at all. Despite that, this find at Wadi Shellaleh was of major importance.

The weather was extremely hot; we measured a temperature in the low 40s (40 degrees centigrade is 104 degrees Fahrenheit). We drove a little farther on, then stopped for lunch under a large acacia tree. Muhammad was still with us, having proved himself a most accurate and dependable guide. After all, Wadi Shellaleh was his own back yard. We gave him a gift for the trouble he had taken with us, and he left us for home, refusing our offer to drive him back. Altogether, he was a most dignified young man.

One thing notable about the Wadi Shellaleh area is a feature it has in common with the other large concentrations of pilgrim inscriptions, Wadi Ḥajjaj and Wadi Mukattab. Each of these sites is a distance of a few kilometers from a water source. For Wadi Shellaleh it is Bir Dakur, for Wadi Ḥajjaj it is 'Ein Ḥudra, and for Wadi Mukattab it is Bir Sheikh Suleiman. This seems to indicate a deliberate pattern. Uzi related that he met a doctor who was doing malaria research in the Sinai. He pointed out that the malaria mosquito is prevalent but that there are few cases of the disease among the bedouin. This is, he thinks, because they will never sleep near a water source, only at some distance. This apparently prevents infection from the mosquitoes. Could it be that the pattern with the pilgrim night stations was similar and that today's bedouin act according to some inherited wisdom?

As I write now I recall one of Felix Fabri's narratives that strikingly confirms our observation. He repeatedly relates that the bedouin guide in charge of their caravan, the Calinus, as he calls him, would absolutely not let him and his party sleep at any water hole. I also recall a comment by an American traveler, Franklin E. Hoskins, early in the twentieth century. In a book published in 1912 he remarked that the Arabs sleep away from water holes for safety.[15] Burckhardt attributes this custom to the danger of being

---

14. The locations described are Rock Inscriptions Project sites Shellal 1–7.

15. *From the Nile to Nebo: A Discussion of the Problem and the Route of the Exodus* (Philadelphia: Sunday School Times, 1912), 192.

waylaid.[16] These were interesting confirmations of the pattern that we had observed from the location of the inscriptional material.

Felix Fabri does not give any reason except to say that his guide did not want to encounter Arabs. Hoskins attributes it to safety. Burckhardt clearly implied the same. Avner Goren, with whom I discussed this matter, pointed out that in earlier times dangerous wild animals were much more numerous and that they would naturally frequent the watering places. Certainly in former times, before they were hunted into extinction, panthers, ostriches, and other wild animals were found in the Sinai. Thus, it seems to me, a number of considerations must have generated this custom—but the need for security and the desire to be free of mosquitoes were probably chief among them. In any case, this pattern is absolutely indubitable.

We set out to return along Wadi Budra at 1:50 PM. Uzi had wished to examine Naqb Budra, for he recalled that the great Egyptologist W. M. Flinders Petrie in his *Researches in Sinai* mentioned inscriptions there.[17] Petrie, predominantly an Egyptologist and a pioneer in archaeological method, came to the Sinai to study the Egyptian turquoise mines of Wadi Maghara and Serabit el-Khadem. So we set off for our next stop, having achieved successfully the main purpose of our journey: to examine the area of Naqb Rakne for inscriptions and to seek the reported concentration of inscriptions in Wadi Abu Natash. While doing this, we discovered the large group of inscriptions in Wadi Shellaleh, one of the largest in the Sinai.

At 2:15 PM we reached the well called Bir Sheikh Suleiman. Here a group of bedouin men were filling a large number of jerry cans with water from the well and loading them on a jeep. They were from Wadi Maghara; we later saw them returning home with their water supplies, for Wadi Maghara has no water source of its own. The well is about 30 meters deep and lined with stones, quite an engineering feat. The changes that modernity has brought to the life of the bedouin are reflected in all sorts of ways. One of them was the sight of the men drawing the water and taking it home in large quantities on a jeep instead of the women carrying it in small quantities by hand or by donkey. Unlike the Arab villagers, the bedouin women did not use pottery jars (or their replacement, the tin can).

---

16. John Lewis Burckhardt, *Travels in Syria and the Holy Land* (London: Murray, 1822), 449, 495.

17. W. M. Flinders Petrie, *Researches in Sinai* (New York: Dutton, 1906). His book is profusely illustrated with photographs.

Instead, they used water skins, carried on their backs, suspended from a band across the forehead, or loaded on donkeys. On the subject of water, we ourselves were dependent on the two jerry cans we had taken with us from Saint Catherine's. Ḥmed asked me once how I could stand not washing all over, since I was used to living in the city, where there was unlimited water.

The topic of water also came up the next day as we drove from the administration buildings at the foot of Jebel Musa to the airfield. Our driver was one of the Mount Sinai bedouin, and we were driving in his own large truck. The conversation turned, as it often did on this trip, to how the bedouin would like the Egyptian rule that was about to be inaugurated. Certainly the bedouin with whom I talked were somewhat wary of the situation that would be created after the Israeli withdrawal. Our driver pointed out that only a few of his tribe had not gone to work for the Israelis in one way or another. He himself intended to go to Eilat, he said, when Saint Catherine's reverted to Egypt. Once one has gone beyond a certain point, he explained, it is impossible to go back. He was referring to his standard of living, of course. Among the examples he adduced, the one on which he expatiated for a long time, was water. He had become used to taking long, hot showers every day and could not think of going back to washing by pouring tiny amounts of water over himself from a tin can. Water—the scarcity of it—is, of course, a central fact of life for the bedouin.

Anyway, by the time we reached Bir Sheikh Suleiman our own water supply was lukewarm. We had taken ice with us, but by the middle of the second day it had all melted, and water in plastic jerry cans quickly turns tepid. Uzi had cooled some at lunchtime by letting it stand in open containers in the shade. The evaporation of the surface level had cooled the water below it somewhat, but this was not much help, and we were glad to fill our insulated water bags with well water, which tasted good enough and was cool.

We turned into Wadi Maghara to visit an acquaintance, the bedouin watchman whom we had met during our previous expedition. He was not in his encampment when we arrived, but we were served tea by his eldest son, who was about ten. The children, and there were about half a dozen of them, had grown up a lot since our last visit. A boy from one of the neighboring families sold me two small pieces of turquoise. These were from the mines in the wadi that had been worked by the ancient Egyptians; the bedouin children still gather small turquoise stones to sell to passing travelers.

As I left, one of the little girls who had apparently taken a liking to me ran after me and gave me another small stone as a gift. We recorded our names in the guest book the watchman keeps. Not too many more Israelis would do that before the Egyptians assumed control again.

Once I returned to Jerusalem I had a Yemenite silversmith whom I knew well set the turquoise stones in silver as earrings for my wife. They were handsome and unusual; I liked the idea of her wearing turquoise from the same mines as the Pharaohs. One day, some years later, our house was burgled, and they were stolen and never recovered. This journal, I hope, will preserve a memory of them and of the adventure of which they were part, for my own memory has no permanence.

SINAI SCENES 10
In Serabit's turquoise mines
I bought two blue-green stones
wrapped in an olive oily cloth,
to make ear-rings for my love.
The masters' hieroglyphs on stelae
and in the mines,
ancient slaves' Semitic.

MES

We followed Wadi Sidri until it ran into Wadi Mukattab and then Wadi Mukattab until it ran into Wadi Feiran, tracing these interlocking wadis back toward Santa Katerina. We drove along the northern side of the broad valley of Wadi Feiran. There we observed fourth-millennium BCE enclosures with standing stones; we had not noticed them before. Such sacred places, marked out with borders of gathered stones, often had standing stones, frequently three in number, at one end. Uzi pointed out that, if one lies down and looks in the direction indicated by the central—usually the highest—of those standing stones, one often sees a lofty mountain peak directly ahead.

In Wadi Feiran we had another puncture. We changed tires again and decided that we would wait to repair the puncture until we got to the bedouin center at Feiran, where there is a garage. We arrived in Feiran in the mid-afternoon, and Ḥmed set about fixing the tire there. The garage

4. THE THIRD EXPEDITION, 16–18 JUNE 1979

was closed because of some problem with the generator, so he had to do the repair by hand. This is common, and repair patches and a manual air pump are standard equipment with a jeep equipped for desert travel. No sooner had he fixed one tire than there was a puncture in another. Then the manual pump broke, and it took all our ingenuity to fix it. Next the rubber tubing that connects the pump to the valve split. Fortunately, this last mishap took place after all the tires were fixed and inflated, but as a result of all this it was almost dark when we left Feiran and quite dark before we were very far en route. However, we had rested a bit and drank cold orange juice at the bedouin cafe there. We also drank coffee with spices that Uzi had cooked on his little portable primus stove as we chatted with Frej, the bedouin who is responsible for the Sinai Development Administration affairs at Feiran. Altogether, it was a pleasant hour.

Another delightful experience happened on the way back to Saint Catherine's. Fathi, who had been our driver on our previous visit and to whom we had become attached, had just gotten married. He lived at a small oasis between Feiran and Saint Catherine's. The bedouin there have built a small building in front of which stands a trellis with abundant grape vines hanging from it. They ran a small café and soft drink store there during the day. When we arrived, it was dark, and only a single kerosene lamp provided light. Fathi, in bedouin dress, a long gown and keffiyeh on his head (not the checked shirt and jeans he had worn as our driver), was sitting on carpets with his father, his father-in-law, and his brother around the ashes of a fire. He received us warmly, and we spent an enjoyable half-hour exchanging news. Descriptions of bedouin life often highlight the role that conversation plays in their society. Now, with the increasing availability of modern technology and electricity, perhaps things are changing.

Lesley Hazelton in her book about the Negev and Sinai describes the north Sinai bedouin, as indeed does every traveler and raconteur of desert life.[18] Hazelton, whose acquaintance was mediated through people who knew them well, points out the different attitudes of the nineteenth- and early twentieth-century travelers toward them and finds herself most in sympathy with the attitude of Charles Montague Doughty, the intrepid Englishman who lived among the bedouin of the Arabian peninsula in the late nineteenth century (fig. 15). He viewed them realistically, neither

---

18. Lesley Hazelton, *Where Mountains Roar: A Personal Report from the Sinai and Negev Desert* (New York: Holt, Rinehart & Winston, 1980).

Fig. 15. Charles Doughty from the frontispiece of the 1926 edition of *Arabia Deserta*

overly romanticizing them nor facilely condemning them as lazy and thieving. Because of the bedouin who worked with us, I took an interest in these very varying descriptions of the Sinai bedouin. In fact, it had been my intention to write at some length about how different writers perceived the bedouin and described them, but Lesley Hazelton preempted me, and most interestingly.

A similarly unromantic but sympathetic view may be found in Wilfred Thesiger's description of his years with the bedouin of the southern Arabian peninsula in the middle of the twentieth century, before the exploitation of oil affected their way of life.[19] Hazelton and writer Burton Bernstein both traveled in search, not of biblical remains, but simply of the desert. Bernstein made several journeys with Clinton Bailey of Tel-Aviv University, and he described them first in the *New Yorker Magazine*. Bailey had worked with and studied the bedouin of Sinai for many years and published a number of books on the subject, one with an introduction by Wilfred Thesiger. Bernstein's description is detailed and sympathetic toward people whom earlier travelers had described as degenerate, lazy, thieving, and generally of no use whatsoever. Each person sees Sinai through the lens of his or her own interest, and mine was basically the perspective of the pilgrims. The desert's impact on me was extraordinary, and Uzi's broad knowledge of so many aspects of the desert and its flora, fauna, and people deepened my perception and profoundly enriched the entire experience.

Upon our eventual arrival at the administration building at Saint Catherine's, we discovered that the place was virtually deserted. We were offered the hospitality of a room, however, and unpacked our gear, then spent some time writing up our notes and getting our materials in order,

---

19. Thesiger, *Arabian Sands*, 319–30.

for we had planned a full program for the next morning right up to the moment when we embarked on the flight back north.

Monday, 18 June 1979

We did not awake as early as the previous day but managed to set out at 6:45 with the goal of rephotographing one of the inscriptions at nearby Wadi Leja. That was successful, and, as a bonus, we found an additional Armenian inscription there. We went farther on into the wadi than Tom and I had penetrated previously. At the end of the wadi near the monastery of Deir El-Arba'in, there are more rocks with large numbers of inscriptions.

I turned back near where the extensive stone-walled olive tree plantations and orchards of the monastery commence. I wished to resurvey the part of the wadi near the new chapel, by the rock that is traditionally identified as that which Moses struck to bring forth water. Meanwhile Uzi pushed on still farther, following the path to the west of the olive groves where there are also some large walnut trees. He found many inscriptions in that area and photographed some Greek ones, together with what he thought was a Georgian graffito. It seems probable that there are additional inscriptions along the paths up Jebel Musa and Jebel Safsafa. Thus a return to the Saint Catherine's region one more time was put on the agenda. We wished to study this area around Deir El-Arba'in, ascend Jebel Musa from that side, and descend on the Saint Catherine's side. Another visit to this area would also enable us to hike through the Naqb el-Hawa Pass, north of the Saint Catherine's area, and go as far as the oasis called Sheikh 'Awad. This was most likely the last stop of pilgrims approaching the monastery from the west. To achieve these aims would doubtless take the best part of a three-day visit.

Wadi Leja was much as I remembered it from my previous visit. Monks had laid the paved path along which we walked, in an age in which such manual work was part of their discipline (fig. 16). In some parts the paving stones were still in place, while in others they were missing; however, the edge, or kerbstones, survived nearly the whole length of the path. Toward the cultivated areas and gardens belonging to Deir El-Arba'in, the path was in better repair. Stone walls surrounded the plantations of olive trees that the bedouin cultivated for the monks.

Numerous Nabatean inscriptions and the curious "footprints" marked into the rock occur all the way along the wadi. The footprints are just that: the outlines of two feet next to each other. Their exact significance is

Fig. 16. Byzantine paving in Wadi Leja

unknown, and we were unable to imagine what it might have been. They did not seem to be Christian, so, we reasoned, the path laid by the monks must have followed an older, Nabatean way. As often in the Sinai, the path ran not on the wadi bed but along the side some meters higher than it to avoid flash floods.

Although there are a few Greek inscriptions between the mouth of the wadi and the start of the cultivated gardens, most of them are to be found near Moses's rock and as far as the monastery of Deir El-Arba'in. Moses's rock is about a kilometer into the wadi. It is approximately 2.5 meters high and patterned with parallel crevices and markings such as one might imagine to have been created by flowing water. They actually result from chemical erosion.

Burckhardt describes it in detail, and not much has changed since the publication of his work in 1822:

> At twenty minutes walk from the Erbayn we passed a block of granite, said to be the rock out of which the water issued when struck by the rod of Moses. It lies quite isolated by the side of the path, which is about ten feet higher than the lowest bottom of the valley. The rock is about twelve feet in height, of an irregular shape approaching a cube. There are some apertures upon its surface, through which the water is

said to have burst out; they are about twenty in number, and lie nearly in a straight line round the three sides of the stone. They are for the most part ten or twelve inches long, two or three inches broad, and from one to two inches deep, but a few of them are as deep as four inches. Every observer must be convinced, on the slightest examination, that most of these fissures are the work of art, but three or four perhaps are natural, and these may have first drawn the attention of the monks to the stone, and have induced them to call it the rock of the miraculous supply of water. Besides the marks of art evident in the holes themselves, the spaces between them have been chiselled, so as to make it appear as if the stone had been worn in those parts by the action of the water; though it cannot be doubted, that if water had flowed from the fissures it must generally have taken quite a different direction. One traveller saw on this stone twelve openings, answering to the number of the tribes of Israel; another describes the holes as a foot deep. They were probably told so by the monks, and believed what they heard rather than what they saw.[20]

I have mentioned the new chapel there; indeed, it was not yet completed. It is a rectangular stone building with a yellow roof, and the corner of Moses's rock is inside the church, to the left of the apse. The chapel is, incidentally, oriented on a north-south axis, with the apse to the south, an unusual orientation. The number of inscriptions increases notably in this part of the wadi, and there are Greek ones, including a couple cut deeply into Moses's rock itself, to the right of the "water marks."

Later that morning we had the opportunity to make a brief visit to Saint Catherine's Monastery. The parts that visitors are permitted to see are the church, which is an impressive basilical structure, and the area around the walls. Many before me have described and photographed the monastery and church. From our particular point of view, it was notable that there were few graffiti both in the long approach to the monastery and, as far as we could tell, within the building itself. We observed some Greek ones on the older of the two pairs of wooden doors at the entrance of the church, those that lead from the narthex into the nave. The Crusader doors leading into the narthex bear the insignia of the craftsmen and a twelfth-century date.

I also examined about half of the outer wall of the monastery for inscriptions. There were stone crosses, mainly standing out in relief, with

---

20. Burckhardt, *Travels in Syria*, 578–79.

their background aligned with the rest of the wall. Most were in the oldest part of the wall. In the narthex of the church is a small display of manuscripts and icons. An Armenian manuscript, apparently of the seventeenth century, was on show there, as well as a Georgian manuscript. In the place of their lost Codex Sinaiticus, taken in the nineteenth century by Constantine von Tischendorf and sold to the czar of Russia, the monks have set a volume of the facsimile of it. A Syriac manuscript dated to the fifth century was displayed upside down. I remarked upon this to the monk keeping watch in the church, but he did not seem particularly interested. The arrival of the Ethiopian bishop of Jerusalem, a new appointee, who came just then to pay his first visit to Saint Catherine's, caused a flurry of excitement. I gathered that the head of the monastery was not available to receive him, so he joined a group of tourists who were receiving an extremely inaccurate explanation about the church in English and German from a professional guide. We continued, however, on our own tour. What I learned from this visit is that without proper introductions and the cooperation of the authorities of Saint Catherine's, the chances of our finding out about Armenians and Armenian pilgrims from sources within the monastery were poor.

The flight home was uneventful. I had a stopover in Eilat, where it was extremely hot, about 43 degrees Celsius (109 Fahrenheit). Jerusalem with its 25 degrees Celsius (77 Fahrenheit) and evening cool was a pleasant contrast. The day after I got home, Tom came by to take his leave; he was departing for Europe and Soviet Armenia. He reported finding three Armenian graffiti at the Basilica of the Annunciation in Nazareth. This was a foreshadowing of later discoveries. The footsteps of the Armenians seem to be clearly discernible at many of the holy places of this country.

5
THE FOURTH EXPEDITION: MOUNT SINAI
23–25 FEBRUARY 1980

After the June trip I was unable to return to the Sinai for eight months. In July and August I worked keenly toward concluding the first draft of the publication of the epigraphs that we had found. I also prepared the intermediate report, which appeared in August 1979.[1] This report was an attempt to pull together the results of our researches up to that time and to draw out some of their historical implications.

I felt that it was important to make the discovery public and to edit and publish the finds promptly. It is often a weakness of archaeological expeditions and fieldwork that their results tend to lie unpublished for years, if not decades. My policy was to produce a preliminary report, followed by a full, scholarly publication, as quickly as possible. I followed the same principle two decades later in my other major archaeological activity, the excavation of the medieval Jewish cemetery in Armenia. The full report of this find was out within a year of conclusion of the excavations.

I had undertaken to go to Philadelphia for three months starting in September 1979 to teach at the University of Pennsylvania. I knew that two chief goals remained for study in Saint Catherine's area. The first was to finish retracing the pilgrims' route past Deir-el-Arba'in and up Jebel Musa (Mount Sinai). The second was to follow up a published report of "scattered Armenian inscriptions" in Saint Catherine's Monastery itself. Moreover, one inscription, supposedly from the Chapel of Elijah on Jebel Musa, had been published some years ago. I was eager to see the original, particularly since I had not yet succeeded in locating the publication.

---

1. Michael E. Stone, *Armenian Inscriptions from Sinai: Intermediate Report with Notes on Georgian and Nabatean Inscriptions* (Sydney: Maitland, 1979).

There were two interesting developments while I was in the United States. I discussed some ideas about the pilgrims' choice of routes with Philip Mayerson of New York University. These stimulated Philip to undertake new research on this subject, and the results of his studies were presented in an article.[2] I eagerly awaited its appearance so that I could read it. Although the article was quite interesting, he did not succeed in solving the problems that I perceived arising from the distribution of the inscriptions.

The second development was that I met with my old friend, the polyglot Belgian monk and scholar, the late Father Michel van Esbroeck, SJ. Father Michel belonged to the Bollandist order of Jesuit monks who, for over two centuries, have studied traditions about the lives of saints of the various Christian churches. He was an expert on Armenian and Georgian and other oriental languages and had been in Jerusalem in the early summer. I asked him then to undertake the publication of the Georgian inscriptions from Wadi Ḥajjaj and Wadi Mukattab. He took the photos and other material back to Brussels, and when we met in early November he was able to tell me that the earliest Georgian inscriptions were from the fifth/sixth centuries, while the latest were seven hundred or more years later. Since the Georgians started to write only in the fourth or fifth century, the antiquity of these inscriptions was as remarkable as that of the Armenian ones. We agreed to publish our results in a joint volume containing the Armenian and Georgian inscriptions from the Sinai.[3] All these developments, together with the wide interest that the inscriptions I had found aroused in America, made me eager to return to the Saint Catherine's area and complete my research.

Under the agreements between Israel and Egypt, the area of Saint Catherine's was to revert to Egyptian rule on 26 January 1980. When I went to the United States in early September 1979, I planned to make the trip

---

2. Philip Mayerson, "The Pilgrim Routes to Mount Sinai and the Armenians," *Israel Exploration Journal* 32 (1982): 44–57. In this study he concluded that, in fact, during the late Roman and early Byzantine times the preferred route for travel from Jerusalem was via Eilat (Aila) and then south through the wadis parallel to the Gulf of Akaba to Mount Sinai. I am not quite sure of this conclusion, but clearly the eastern route was more prominent than was previously thought. Our discovery of the Armenian inscriptions catalyzed this changed perspective.

3. M. E. Stone, ed., *The Armenian Inscriptions from the Sinai*, with appendixes on the Georgian and Latin Inscriptions by Michel van Esbroeck and W. Adler, Harvard Armenian Texts and Studies 6 (Cambridge: Harvard University Press, 1982).

5. THE FOURTH EXPEDITION, 23–25 FEBRUARY 1980

south to study the inscriptions fairly soon after my return in mid-November, well before the 26 January deadline. This would have been a simple matter; Avner Goren could easily have helped me with travel and a guide, and all I needed was two days at the most. Nevertheless, political events, particularly in the Middle East, have a way of upsetting the best-laid plans. While I was in Philadelphia, I heard that Prime Minister Begin as a special gesture to President Sadat of Egypt had agreed to withdraw from the Saint Catherine's area two months early, in fact, a day or two before I came home from Philadelphia. After the area came under the Egyptian rule, the situation was unclear for some time. An interim period lasted until 26 January 1980, the date originally established for the return of that area to the Egyptians. Up to that date the Egyptian authorities allowed Israeli citizens to cross the border freely; after that date Israelis were to be permitted to cross the border only upon presenting valid passports. This arrangement was in force even as the negotiations between Israel and Egypt moved toward a normalization of travel between the two countries.

Between my return in mid-November and the last week of December, various circumstances prevented me from undertaking the arrangements for my trip. Late in December I started what turned out to be a lengthy series of discussions with the authorities. Eventually I talked with Brigadier-General Dov Sión, the Israeli chairman of the joint Israel-Egypt military committee. He told me that on 10 January 1980, in the context of the committee's work, there was to be a meeting between representatives of the Israeli universities and those of the University of Ismailia. I hoped that my request would be presented to the Egyptians at that meeting and that I would hear from the committee of its approval. That evening I talked with Professor Emmanuel Neumaier, who was the Hebrew University representative on that committee. I heard that, instead of discussing specific requests from Israeli scholars and scientists whose work in the Sinai had been cut off by the return of the territory to Egypt, the meeting was devoted to matters of a more general character. This was disappointing news for me and for the others as well. I spoke again with General Sión, however, who put me in touch with Avraham Shaked of the Society for the Protection of Nature in Israel.

Shaked, as he is called, was most helpful. He undertook to provide me with a guide who had been a member of the field school at Saint Catherine's before the withdrawal. The Nature Protection Society had operated the field school, and it was one of the groups still authorized to guide tours in the Saint Catherine's area. My discussions with Shaked and other preparations soon stretched beyond the 26 January date. It seemed to us that the nature of my research scarcely extended beyond that of a visitor interested in any particular aspect of the area. I intended, after all, only to copy and photograph any inscription I saw and certainly not to touch, change, or harm them in any way. Thus I proceeded to plan for a trip to Saint Catherine's area, even though my official request had not yet been approved. In the end, it was approved on Friday, 22 February, the day before I left.

Saturday, 23 February 1980

I talked with Michal Shefer, who was our guide, a number of times on the telephone but did not meet her until she boarded our taxi on Saturday, 23 February, at 6:15 AM. Michal was as keen as I was to revisit the Saint Catherine's area. She had lived and worked there at the Tzukei David Field School (its official name) for three and a half years, leaving only on the last day of Israeli administration. In her time there she had learned bedouin Arabic and had made numerous friends among the Sinai bedouin; her desire was not just to visit well-loved sites but also to visit friends there and see how they were faring under the Egyptian dispensation. Indeed, throughout our time there, whenever Michal had a spare hour or so she was always invited to visit one or another family or friend. On one of these visits, she saw Fathi and brought me news and greetings from him. More than this, Michal turned out to be an excellent guide. She knew every inch of the territory, every plant, the name of every peak and wadi. We were much indebted, as will emerge below, to her experience and extensive acquaintances among the bedouin and among the monks of the monastery. We soon discovered that she had physical endurance to outdistance the two of us, and she sustained a regular, tireless pace both up mountains and down them.

The third member of the party was Bill Adler, a visiting graduate student from the University of Pennsylvania. Bill had studied some Armenian and was pursuing research on Byzantine historical sources. Therefore, he eagerly seized the opportunity to visit this ancient Byzantine monastery as well as the unique adventure of a few days exploring the Sinai area (fig. 17).

Having recruited the members of our group, I began the careful planning of the trip. As indicated, I intended to travel as a visitor and to look for the inscriptions as I toured the area. Here I came to appreciate the help that Uzi and Avner Goren had always given me. My initial plan was to depart on Sunday, 17 February, for a day or two. A phone call soon dis-

5. THE FOURTH EXPEDITION, 23–25 FEBRUARY 1980

Fig. 17. Bill Adler at Saint Catherine's new hostel, 1980

abused me of this idea. Up to 26 January, Arkia, Israel's inland airline, had flown to Mount Sinai airport quite frequently. After that they flew only on Saturdays and Tuesdays. Moreover, the flight took place only if a group of tourists on one of their own package tours was booked onto the plane. Since such a group often filled the small planes completely, we needed a day on which there was a group but also three empty seats. It turned out that we could get confirmed bookings only for Saturday, 23 February, returning the next Tuesday. Even these places were confirmed only on the preceding Thursday afternoon. On Friday morning I set out to buy the food for the three of us. We could sleep in the monastery hostel, but I had been told that there was no food available there. I bought too much, as it turned out, and packed it all up in two cartons, to which I added the photographic equipment and a minimum of clothing. One thing I was grateful to have taken was a flashlight: it turned out to be crucial for reading certain inscriptions.

I beat the alarm and awoke at 5:15 Saturday morning. The taxi arrived promptly at 6:00. I had been concerned about the taxi since it was the Sabbath, and many of the taxi companies do not operate. The timetable was tight, for on Friday the airline had called to tell me that the flight was departing half an hour earlier than had been scheduled. Bill was waiting on his appointed corner at 6:05, and Michal easily found us at the rendezvous at 6:15. She seemed taciturn at first, but as the plane made its way further south her spirits improved, although she was never a talkative companion.

Affairs at Jerusalem's Atarot Airport were much as they had been on our previous trips. There were only Arkia flights and one white UN plane on the tarmac. The coffee shop was closed because of the Sabbath. We moved quickly through airlines and security checks and after a smooth flight (and a good breakfast) found ourselves at the Mount Sinai airport. Again!

I approached the matter of the border crossing with a certain amount of apprehension. First, I had never been to Egypt before. More significant, we were one of the first groups of people to come since January 26 not traveling on a guided tour that arrived and left on the same day. As it happened, all of my apprehensions were needless. Michal's fluent Arabic moved us smoothly through the Egyptian authorities. The Tourist Police took our passports and gave us a form in their stead. This was embellished on the back with several dollars' worth of revenue stamps; it served as our identity paper until we left. As it turned out, no one ever asked for it. I then had to change some more dollars into Egyptian pounds to pay another fee to the Tourist Police, and more stamps were stuck on the forms. This all sounds worse than it was. The only odd thing was that at the bank branch at the airfield (Misbank) there was a large notice listing perhaps twenty currencies and their rates of exchange. The Israeli lira was not among them. Perhaps this was some fault in adjustment to the new situation, or perhaps it was that the wild inflation rate of the Israeli lira (pound) at that time defied any attempt to post its rate of exchange. Indeed, on 24 February, the day after we arrived at Saint Catherine's, the Israeli lira ceased to exist and was replaced by the sheqel.

At about the same time as our plane landed, another arrived from Cairo; we were to see some of the Egyptian and other tourists it brought from Cairo that evening in the hostel. The Egyptians ran very nice Mercedes Benz buses between the airport and the monastery. The one we set out to board was marked ISISTOURS. We looked around for our baggage, but it was nowhere to be seen. The border formalities had been smoother than anticipated, but the Egyptians were not used to people coming on Arkia for more than one day. Therefore, the airport authorities had not checked the plane's baggage compartment. It took only a few moments. A smiling man rode out to the plane on a little cart and brought all but one of our packages. His smile was not affected by the fact that he had to ride out a second time to bring the missing carton. Indeed, he insisted on putting this last, recalcitrant carton of food on the bus himself.

5. THE FOURTH EXPEDITION, 23–25 FEBRUARY 1980

We had left an overcast Jerusalem and arrived to a clear, blue sky and a warm winter's day in the Sinai. We were expecting cold weather—Michal had warned us to take snow gear. I had not even taken a sun hat, just a woolen snow hat. The run to the monastery from the airport was a familiar one for Michal and me. The only new thing I noticed was a sandbagged Egyptian defense point set up by the road along the way. Some of the dust of the Sinai penetrated the bus as we rode the unpaved part of the road, but this was the only touch of it on this visit. The Hebrew parts of all the road signs had been covered over with black paint, and some new signs in English and Arabic had been erected.

The bus unloaded us at the outer gate of the monastery. We were all fairly burdened, and we enviously watched the group of tourists with their light hand bags proceed up the ascent toward the monastery. Michal had immediately spotted friends among the bedouin who were at the gate of the monastery, and one of them had a camel that would carry our packages for a fee. So all the gear, including my photographic equipment, was loaded into the camel's saddlebags, and we followed its swaying gait up to the monastery. We did not go to the lower entrance but around to the side. The monks had decided to direct the traffic through the side doorway, which tourists had to use.

A number of bedouin were gathered around the side doorway. Some of them wanted to sell us crystalline stones. This was different from my previous visits there and was, I gather, a result of the drop in employment opportunities under the Egyptian administration.

Broad, gradual steps led up to the side gateway into the compound: a nineteenth-century construction of the same type as the bell tower inside. The bell tower, a donation by Czar Alexander II of Russia (1855–1881), was built in 1871 and holds nine bells.

We sat on the steps, Bill and I, while Michal went off to find the monk Father Sophronius, a good friend of hers. The camel and its bedouin driver waited with us. Suddenly from the height of three stories or so, a monk put his head out of a window (later I realized that it was Father Sophronius) and directed a flow of Arabic at the camel driver. Then another deluge of words descended on him from the same source. Father Sophronius suddenly disappeared, and a bedouin head appeared from the same window, smiling broadly. As far as I could gather, our driver was being rebuked for bringing his camel up to that particular point and being directed to go around to the lower gate. He did not seem greatly disturbed by the whole event, and when Michal returned to tell us that all was in order and that we had a room in the hostel, he then proceeded calmly through the gate with his camel and unloaded our packages by the steps leading down to the new hostel the monks had recently finished constructing.

Michal's attachment to the Sinai bedouin was potent. I had learned something about the bedouin during my previous visits and came to appreciate and admire those whom I encountered. As I already mentioned, the impact of the Egyptian administration on the bedouin was already starting to be felt when we made our visit. Many of the sources of employment available under Israeli rule dried up, which made them once again dependent on the monastery. The symbiosis between the bedouin and the monks is an odd one. Justinian originally built the monastery fortress to protect the monks against bedouin incursions. At various times in the history of the monastery, the bedouin had threatened the monks; at others, they were dependent on them. The mosque inside the monastery with its tall tower witnesses a zenith of bedouin power. Now, with many sources of income dried up, many bedouin sat around the monastery gates idle or trying to sell rocks to the tourists.

It was 10:00 AM. We proceeded to our room, which we had to ourselves. It was furnished with six two-tiered beds, each of which was provided with two sheets, a pillow, and a blanket. The only other furnishings were two straight-backed chairs (fig. 18). The hostel is quite a handsome building, covered with wild stone and reminiscent of the Israeli buildings throughout the Sinai. The metal doors to the rooms were arched and surmounted by a cross set in a little window. There was also a single window to the room and a large opening between the bottom of the door and the plain concrete floor. I attributed this opening to some slipup in the course of construction. The washrooms were at the other end of the row of rooms; to reach them one had to walk through the courtyard past all the other rooms, each with its window and little peephole in the door. The kitchen (with a gas stove and a sink) was in the middle of the row. The problem of privacy was resolved in a simple fashion. The monastery's source of electric power is a generator, which they turn on at dusk and turn off at 9:30 PM. After that, it was dark, with all the darkness of a world in which there is no artificial light at all.

We dumped our gear in the room and decided to set forth without delay to survey the area between Wadi el-Deir and Wadi Leja on foot. We left the monastery through the side door; the route stretched back from behind the building. It started as an easy ascent on the well-made path, which continued all the way up the mountain. Abbas Pasha, the viceroy

5. THE FOURTH EXPEDITION, 23–25 FEBRUARY 1980

Fig. 18. Our room in the hostel at Saint Catherine's

of Egypt 1849–1854, laid this path to give access to the mountain where he planned to build a palace. Eventually he built the palace elsewhere. This brings to mind the comments of nineteenth-century travelers who report that this mountainous area was regarded as being particularly beneficial to one's health. Palmer tells the following curious anecdote about Viceroy Abbas Pasha, who took recourse to doctors after his indulgent life of debauchery affected his health. His medical advisers counseled him to see whether the desert air would have a beneficial influence on him, so he came and took up residence in Saint Catherine's Monastery. Palmer continues:

> Feeling the beneficial effects of the pure mountain air, he determined to build a palace in the neighbourhood; and in order to ascertain which was the most healthy location he adopted the following original expedient. Joints of fresh meat were exposed on all accessible mountain-tops around, and that on which the flesh should remain for the longest time without corruption was to be declared the healthiest spot. But ... his highness changed his viceregal mind and ... decided to dwell upon the holy mountain itself, so as to enjoy the benefit of Moses' especial protection.... a road was commenced [and] this again was abandoned, and the road now known as "the Pasha's Road" was ultimately constructed ... and still forms the most convenient approach to the summit.[4]

---

4. Edward H. Palmer, *The Desert of the Exodus: Journeys on Foot in the Wilderness of the Forty Years' Wanderings* (Cambridge: Deighton & Bell, 1871), 132–33. Writing of supplies to carry in the desert, Agnes Smith Lewis relates the following: "Eggs

We continued up Abbas Pasha's path, and as we advanced the ascent became more difficult. The way zigzagged up the side of the mountain, parts of it being quite steep. Michal treated the climb as if it did not exist, but Bill and I found it tiring.

Quite a considerable way up, I would estimate over half of the ascent, was a large new stone plaque with an English inscription on it from the book of Deuteronomy. We did not expect to find many of the pilgrim inscriptions, if indeed any, on this path, since it was relatively new. About 50 meters down from the large plaque, however, we did find a Greek inscription. As we examined this and the stone plaque, we observed a white chapel on the peak opposite us. That peak was Jebel Moneijat (Mount of Meeting), where, according to tradition, Moses and Jethro met and held their lively discussions, as the book of Exodus reports (18:5–23).

The stone plaque and Greek inscription on Jebel Musa seemed to be about the same elevation as the peak of Jebel Moneijat, and the zigzag path up that mountain was clearly visible. As we observed Jebel Moneijat, to its right we saw another mountain, Jebel Adir, on the side of which another white building nestled. This, Michal told us, was a hermitage inhabited by a Greek solitary monk who had been there about ten years. I questioned her about inscriptions on these two sites. She was quite positive that there were none notable at the hermitage and only Greek on the peak of Jebel Moneijat. Our vague hopes of reaching these two sites were not fulfilled, but to judge from the situation we discovered at Deir el-Arba'in the following day, the chances of finding Armenian there were slight.

There are many descriptions of Jebel Musa and the surrounding mountains, which were the object of the quest of many travelers in the nineteenth century and earlier. Jebel Musa is the peak at the southeastern end of a mountain ridge, and the rest of the ridge running roughly northwest is Jebel Safsafa. Tradition identifies Jebel Safsafa as Mount Horeb. Research carried out by the field school uncovered an extensive pattern of monastic settlement on Jebel Safsafa, centering in three high valleys on the mountain massif. The pilgrims coming from Wadi Leja in all probability ascended Jebel Safsafa and proceeded from there to the southeast toward

---

were carried packed in common salt, and they remained fresh to the very last, though when we tried the same process at Cambridge they all went bad. The desert air keeps everything sweet longer than it would be elsewhere" (*In the Shadow of Sinai: A Story of Travel and Research from 1895 to 1897* [Cambridge: Cambridge University Press, 2012], 28).

5. THE FOURTH EXPEDITION, 23–25 FEBRUARY 1980

Jebel Musa. Michal had been one of those working on the survey of Jebel Safsafa led by Avner Goren and Israel Finkelstein of Tel-Aviv University. She was quite certain that, except for the Chapel of Elijah, they had found no inscriptions on Jebel Safsafa.

By this time we had reached the elevation of the saddle at the head of Wadi Leja. We had a choice: either continue up Jebel Musa and survey the rest of the path and the peak or proceed toward Wadi Leja and complete the survey of that wadi and the ways that led from it to Jebel Musa. This was our original plan. Michal pointed out, however, that the ascent from Wadi Leja, although longer, was not so steep, so we could readily do it the next day. On the other hand, she thought that it would be a pity to lose the elevation on Jebel Musa that we had already achieved. We decided, therefore, to tackle Wadi Leja the next day and to continue immediately up Jebel Musa. The ascent was very steep for the next twenty minutes or so, and I, for one, found it to require considerable physical effort.

The configuration of the mountain is as follows: the first part of the ascent covers a rock-strewn slope that gradually steepens; suddenly the slope ceases, and the peak of the mountain becomes visible. It looks as if it was extruded as a massive single piece of rock. It has perpendicular sides several hundred feet high, which are scored with vertical channels, folds, and crevices running from top to bottom. From this distance, the chapel at the peak of Jebel Musa looks like a matchbox on the top of the mountain. Abbas Pasha's path leads up to the base of the great mass of rock. It then follows a route through a steep defile that Abbas Pasha had blasted in the side of the mountain, as bizarre at that sounds today (fig. 19).

We climbed to the top of the steep rocky slope, where there was shade cast by the

Fig. 19. The author mounting the defile on Abbas Pasha's path

perpendicular cliff above us. At about 12:15 we stopped for lunch at the junction of the slope and the peak. We sorely needed the rest and took about half an hour to eat and refresh ourselves. As we lunched, I looked over at the chapel on Jebel Moneijat, which was now well below us, tiny and quite remote.

After lunch we mounted the narrow defile, which debouched above a valley high in the mountain but some distance below us. The valley into which we looked from the top of the defile is associated with the prophet Elijah and thus called the Vale of Elijah; the building we saw was the Chapel of Elijah. From this point we could see flights of ravens over the peak of the mountain, adding some color to the association of Elijah with this area, for 1 Kgs 17:6 reports that he was fed by ravens, and that took place, according to tradition, in the Vale of Elijah.

We were mounting the famous stairs that lead up the mountain to its peak. In the Byzantine period the monks had laid these steps, which start at the very foot of the mountain. They are made of irregular stones with flat upper surfaces. They form a steep path, but the most direct one, from Saint Catherine's Monastery to the peak of Jebel Musa. Here ended the way that Abbas Pasha had made, so we took up the ancient pilgrim path.

In the Vale of Elijah are a spring and some green trees. Otherwise, the only plants we observed on the mountain were small, growing in the crevices of the rocks. This was so all the way up the mountain as well as on our descent, although the vegetation was more plentiful on the way by which we descended.

At this point we consolidated the water remaining in our canteens and drank quite a bit of it. The danger of dehydration is constant in this dry climate. Unlike the following days, that Saturday the weather was very warm. I had slung my coat below the backpack, which contained the camera gear, and I did not don it until toward evening. By the time we finished lunch and the water, it was nearly 1:00 PM. We decided to split up to make the most efficient use of our time. The well at Elijah's Chapel is one of the three water sources on Jebel Safsafa. Michal planned to take the empty canteens there to fill them. Bill and I would continue to the peak. We fixed a rendezvous at the same spot for 4:30 PM, allotting an hour and a half for the descent from there to the monastery. By 6:00 PM it would be dark. This plan allowed for some time to examine the inscriptions in the Vale of Elijah and by the steps from there down to the monastery.

We stowed some of our gear behind rocks at the foot of the steps, and Bill and I started to climb. The ascent was steep, but I did not find

5. THE FOURTH EXPEDITION, 23–25 FEBRUARY 1980

this part of it as difficult as I had the slope up from Wadi el-Deir to the Abbas Pasha defile. There was snow by the sides of the path and in shaded areas, but the sun was strong and hot, and we both were sunburned. As we ascended, the strain of the climb took its toll; I was tired, but a generous measure of excitement and anticipation offset my fatigue. The experience as we climbed the ancient steps toward the peak was quite unique. There were scattered inscriptions, and one of them seemed to be most probably Armenian, so I photographed and measured it. Indeed, examination at home confirmed my guess, and this became S Arm 1, that is, Mount Sinai Armenian Inscription number 1 in our corpus. All the way up the mountain, the views and vistas that opened up to us were spectacular. That which awaited us at the mountain's peak was extraordinary. To one side we could clearly see the escarpment of the Tih; to the other, the mountains of central and southern Sinai. Michal later told me that she had climbed Jebel Katerina and from there had seen the Red Sea clearly.

As I now look back at the hours that Bill and I spent on the peak of the mountain, I realize that I must have been very fatigued, but I did not feel it then. The steps ascend steeply, and suddenly you are at the summit. Immediately ahead, when you stop at the head of the stairs to catch your breath, is a chapel surrounded by an iron railing. To its right is another square building, which is a mosque today, although it was previously a chapel. The present chapel was constructed in the twelfth century, and both buildings are made of the same sort of reddish granite as the walls of Saint Catherine's Monastery.

Our first discovery of inscriptions at the peak was on a flat rock to the left of the path. An exceptionally clear and large Armenian inscription immediately caught our attention. Archbishop Norayr Bogharian of the Armenian Patriarchate of Jerusalem had published this inscription from a photograph in 1966. We immediately observed another one on this same rock, as well as Greek inscriptions. As I was photographing the second inscription, I noticed yet a third one in faint letters just below it on the rock. The excitement of discovery dispelled whatever fatigue I felt (fig. 20).

I did not record a conscious account of this complex of feelings at the time. When I got the film back from the photographer, the photos were not of the quality I had expected. On the mountain, as I worked, I repeatedly found the settings on the camera to be inexact; my only explanation for this is that, despite my excitement, fatigue was impairing my work. I was grateful for the extensive experience I had had previously in working on

Fig. 20. Bill Adler working on the peak of Jebel Musa

inscriptions. It was invaluable in ensuring that our notes were complete. Still, if another occasion to repeat this climb offers, I will not ascend Jebel Musa on the day I arrive from Jerusalem.

That first inscription dated from the year 1463. Archbishop Bogharian's research showed that its authors were a group of clerics who belonged to the Armenian Patriarchate of Jerusalem, two of whom subsequently became Patriarchs. This inscription is different from all the other inscriptions that we found on Mount Sinai or elsewhere in the Sinai Peninsula. It is dated, easily read, and we can identify the persons involved. While I was photographing it and the others on this rock, Bill was off looking at the church for more.

I found what looked to me to be an Armenian inscription on a rock just inside the side gate in the church fence. I carefully photographed and measured it, but it remained unclear to me. When I later examined the photographs, I concluded that I had been mistaken and that the inscription was in Greek, as were a number of inscriptions on the walls of the chapel. As I was examining them, a shout from Bill alerted me to a group of three inscriptions he had found on a rock between the chapel and the mosque. As I made my way toward him, I made what turned out to be our chief find. At the end of the mosque that faces the chapel, a set of steps leads down

5. THE FOURTH EXPEDITION, 23–25 FEBRUARY 1980

below ground level to a sort of small grotto filled with rubbish. The grotto is a Muslim sacred spot, and the bedouin burn incense there on Eid Al-Adha, one of the chief Muslim feasts. The smoke from the incense has blackened the rock upon which the wall of the mosque is founded and which is clearly visible from the ground level. It was on this rock that I found thirteen more Armenian inscriptions. Some of them were faint, others tiny. This was, however, a concentration of material comparable only to that of Wadi Ḥajjaj. The inscriptions were nearly all simple graffiti just giving names. One or two of them added formulas such as "God have mercy on...."

SINAI SCENES 11
"God have mercy on my camel and guide,"
wrote a pilgrim
on the peak of Jebel Musa.
It is there
with a Greek chapel,
a Georgian inscription,
the soot of bedouin sacrifices.

The holy mountain,
Moses', so they say.
Anyway, it could have been.

MES

Like those in Wadi Ḥajjaj, these graffiti seem to have been executed by pilgrims of no particular distinction. In their general character, they strongly resemble that collection, but judging from the style of writing, I reckoned that some of them were later than the bulk of the Wadi Ḥajjaj material.

Because of the physical location of the inscriptions and the fact that the rock had blackened, it proved difficult to identify, measure, read, transcribe, and photograph them. I did the best I could, and Bill was of great help with the measuring and general physical descriptions. The shortness of time started to press upon us. It was after 3:00 when I finished my first study of this rock and its treasures. By now, it was getting chilly. Bill had left his coat down by the rendezvous and was suffering from the cold. As I worked on the rock under the mosque, he had been exploring further. He found another inscription on another foundation rock of the mosque, at the back near the corner. I checked the inscriptions on the grotto rock, then moved around to the others Bill had found. We soon transcribed, measured, and photographed them. A further search in the environs of the mosque turned up yet another flat rock on which three more Armenian inscriptions had been incised.

At about 3:45 PM we left the summit of Mount Sinai and made our way down the steps to the rendezvous. Michal reached it at the same time. She had found the well at the Chapel of Elijah to be dry and had ranged far over Jebel Safsafa looking for water. In the meanwhile, she had verified her memory that there were no inscriptions on Jebel Safsafa, which had proved accurate. She had also surveyed the area of the Chapel of Elijah and led us down there without further delay. We were soon down in the Vale of Elijah. The chapel was locked, as that on the peak of Mount Sinai had been. There are numerous inscriptions in this general area, most of them Greek and some very recent. One records the visit of travelers from Boston in the nineteenth century. Many of the inscriptions are quite large.

We checked all the points at which Michal had seen inscriptions. In one place I photographed what seemed to me likely to be a Georgian inscription; later, in the course of studying the photographs of the grotto rock on the peak of Mount Sinai, I found another possible Georgian inscription. Here, however, we did not find any as clear or as bold as those we had found in Wadi Ḥajjaj and Wadi Mukattab. Some years later, a student of mine, Bill Whitney, from Harvard, climbed Jebel Musa, and in a valley branching off from the Vale of Elijah he found a number of additional Armenian inscriptions.

We set out down the steps from the Vale of Elijah toward the monastery somewhat after 4:00. Two gates, or rather arches, span the path of the descent, which is unrelenting stairs all the way. Just past one of the arches I found another Armenian inscription on a rock to the left of the path. We photographed it and continued descending. At the second gate, Michal stopped and called my attention to an inscription in Latin characters, AMID or AMIR, on a flat rock face just at the gate. As I looked at it, I suddenly spotted an Armenian inscription, SARGIS, on the same rock. Beautifully incised, it was unique in that it was vertical instead of being horizontal. At its base and to the left of it was a finely drawn human hand, pointing, so it seemed, to the inscription. We photographed that and one more inscription on the descent. The second one turned out to be irrelevant to our search. By now the dusk affected the photography; in addition, Bill and I were rather tired.

5. THE FOURTH EXPEDITION, 23–25 FEBRUARY 1980

About halfway down from the Vale of Elijah is a chapel and what used to be a hermitage. Some writing that seemed, at first glance, to be Armenian held us there for a moment, but it proved to be a false hope. We continued the descent. There were Greek inscriptions by the steps all the way down to well below the second arch, but they petered out beyond the hermitage or chapel.

Other than the Egyptian soldiers who passed us as we ascended, the only people we had seen were a group of about half a dozen German tourists who were mounting just when we met Michal above the Vale of Elijah. They were moving energetically, and one of the women had an infant on her back as they climbed up the steps. We saw them again that evening at Saint Catherine's hostel.

The vegetation was relatively plentiful in the area below the chapel. Striking among the plants I noticed on the descent was one whose leaves were a strong yellow color, which stood out as it was wedged into a crevice on the rock face: the *Verbascum sinaticum*, a plant for which there are no recorded uses. On the peak of the mountain we had seen little rodents that looked to us like mice; that evening I asked Michal about them. They are particular to the desert regions of the Sinai and the area south of the Dead Sea watershed. Called *Acomys russatus*, they live on the highest peaks of the Sinai and in similar environments in Egypt and in the Arabian Peninsula. Naturally, they have the physical characteristics necessary for desert survival. They are a daytime animal and cohabit in desert regions with another variety of acomys that is nocturnal. These small animals can survive on Jebel Musa because of the spring in the Vale of Elijah.

The steps, which the monks built in the Byzantine period, are remarkably well preserved. Stones have fallen aside at a few spots, but the monks of old did an enduring job, as they had done with the path we had trod in Wadi Leja. When we reached the lower part of the descent, we could see Saint Catherine's Monastery between the shoulders of the defile down which the steps had been laid. It made a striking miniature picture that gradually grew larger before our eyes.

We were in our rooms in the hostel soon after 5:00 PM. Michal left immediately for the bedouin village to visit friends, but Bill and I were content to wash up, prepare some food, and relax. The room turned out to have one major drawback: it was terribly cold. So, after we had eaten and rested somewhat, I climbed into my sleeping bag and started to work on the inscriptions and to pull together my notes of the day's activities. It was tolerably warm when one wore three or four layers of clothing, supplemented by a sleeping bag and a blanket or two of those supplied by the monks. Before darkness fell upon us at 9:30 PM, when the generator was turned off, I cleaned and checked the photographic gear, as I did every day in the field.

Sunday, 24 February 1980

After the discoveries of the first day, it seemed to me to unlikely that we would find anything as exciting during the remainder of this stay. Still, we did have the rest of Wadi Leja to check, and on a previous visit Uzi had seen what he thought might be a Georgian inscription there. This was an easy day's walk, however, so we allowed ourselves to take it gradually in the morning. We did not rise until 8:00 and set out for Wadi Leja only at 9:30. Sunday was much colder than Saturday had been. With breakfast, we had tea flavored with rosebuds of a particular type used by the bedouin. This Michal brought with her, having laid in a stock of it when she left Saint Catherine's some months before. I drank similar tea with the bedouin in Wadi Maghara during the previous expedition to western Sinai. This morning's route would lead us by the field school, which had been Michal's home for some years. It being Sunday, the monastery was closed, so we planned to do our work there the next day.

We set off down Wadi el-Deir and around the western base of Jebel Safsafa toward Wadi Leja. As we left the region of Saint Catherine's Monastery, we saw bedouin converging on the monastery from all directions. It was Sunday, so the monastery was closed to visitors; however, on Sundays the bedouin received supplies from the monks. This was part of the somewhat uneasy coexistence between the monastery and the bedouin.

In the distance we could see the buildings that had housed the Israeli administration and the clinic. I questioned Michal and learned that Egyptians were operating the clinic and were using the administration buildings as well. The field school, however, had no fixed inhabitants and was occupied only by a watchman. As we went around Jebel Safsafa, we came across some bedouin women with their goats. They quickly veiled themselves at our approach, and Michal had a lively conversation with them composed chiefly of social formalities. All through Wadi Leja we heard the calls of these girls and women, and some accosted us later to ask for cigarettes. Not being smokers, we could not oblige them.

We quickly picked up the Byzantine path through Wadi Leja. Michal left us to go over to the field school and did not rejoin us until much later.

We set a rendezvous with her at Deir el-Arba'in, the Monastery of the Forty Martyrs. Bill and I worked our way along this wadi, which by now I knew rather well. I showed him the inscriptions we had found there, and I looked for the Thamudic inscription I had seen there six months before. I wanted to photograph it for Joseph Naveh in Jerusalem, but I had not taken my exact notations of it with me, and the memory is deceptive. Consequently, I missed it. On previous occasions I had been into the wadi as far as the start of the olive groves that surround the monastery of Deir el-Arba'in. At this point the wadi, which had been narrow and overshadowed by the great mountains Jebel Safsafa and Jebel Katerina, widened. The monastery itself is a rectangular whitewashed building. There is a rough-stone extension and, of course, the inevitable bedouin encampment.

As we waited by the monastery for Michal's arrival, I searched for the inscription that Uzi had seen. Eventually I found it on a black stone, to the right of the path, a short distance beyond the monastery building. It was of four letters, which I guessed might be Coptic. I photographed it, and, on my return to Jerusalem, some experts read it as the Coptic form of the name Enoch, which confirmed my guess. Coptic writing is an adapted form of the Greek alphabet, but is usually quite distinct in appearance from Greek. I have not noticed any Coptic inscriptions elsewhere in the Sinai or at Mount Sinai itself, except for this one. Other scholars who examined the photograph, however, were skeptical about its being Coptic, so something of a mystery remains. It would, of course, be no surprise to find Coptic. We know of Coptic-speaking Egyptian monks who withdrew to Mount Sinai at the beginnings of monasticism in Egypt. Indeed, when one considers the geographical situation, the absence of Coptic is rather surprising.

While we were awaiting Michal by the monastery of Deir el-Arba'in, bedouin children beset us. They appeared out of ramshackle huts leaning up against the monastery wall and showed great interest in us. They watched intently as Bill changed the film in his camera. Soon Michal joined us. She had tarried at the field school, where she had met some Egyptian researchers from Ismailia.

With our group once again together, we continued along the stretch between Deir el-Arba'in Monastery and the saddle. The path we were following eventually joins the Abbas Pasha path that we had ascended the day before. Today's climb was not as steep as that, and the terrain had also changed. Instead of the narrow, rocky wadi we had traversed as far as the monastery of Deir el-Arba'in, we were now on the slope of Mount Sinai, climbing and overlooking a broad valley. The path had a sheer drop on the right, while on the left were stone formations of a reddish rock that, as it had cooled in ages past, had cracked into bizarre square and polygonal formations, stacked one on the other like a giant child's building blocks. My experience in the Sinai is that this sort of rock rarely served for inscriptions; indeed, between Deir el-Arba'in and the spot where we ate our lunch we found only one or two Greek inscriptions and a few crosses. The Byzantine path that we were following was in good repair. The large kerbstones and nearly all the flat paving stones were in place.

One of the most remarkable features of the Mount Sinai area is the industry of the Byzantine monks. They must have populated this area quite thickly, since they invested enormous energies in the building of paths, chapels, steps, and other projects. A survey carried out by Israel Finkelstein and Avner Goren on Jebel Safsafa uncovered the extraordinary extent of settlement on that mountain. Although the path in Wadi Leja was Byzantine, it was not the chief route used by the ancient pilgrims. Finkelstein and Goren's survey had shown that there were three other paths ascending from Deir el-Arba'in to Jebel Safsafa and from there to Mount Sinai. Michal assured me that these paths contained no inscriptions, and her survey of Jebel Safsafa on Saturday had already confirmed this. The only place on these paths where we saw inscriptions was the Vale of Elijah. There is a rock with a Greek inscription on it opposite Deir el-Arba'in; there an acomys ran right across our path.

The extensive olive groves of the monastery of Deir el-Arba'in were below us, while the rest of the landscape was barren. Except for the bedouin women shepherding their flocks high on the mountainside and the children who supervised Bill when he changed the film, we met no one from the time we entered Wadi Leja about 10:00 AM until we returned to Saint Catherine's Monastery at 2:30 PM.

We climbed for about twenty or thirty minutes until we reached the saddle itself. The weather was chilly, and all Sunday I walked in my parka. At the saddle we took shelter from the cold winter weather behind some rocks. It was the middle of the day, so we decided to eat lunch there. We enjoyed the sandwiches we had prepared, finishing up with some unshelled Sinai almonds that Michal had brought the previous evening. We cracked them open with a rock, and they had an exceptionally fine flavor. This variety is typical to the Sinai, we were told, and the bedouin prize it.

By our luncheon spot, almost at the top of the saddle, we observed a large rock. We had followed a steep path that branched off the Byzantine trail to the right. The large rock held a number of Nabatean inscriptions, the first inscriptions of any importance we had seen after those at Deir-el-Arba'in. The contrast with the situation in Wadi Leja was stark, and we puzzled over this location of Nabatean inscriptions. The mystery remained as acute as it had been before.

At this point we separated. Michal headed back through Wadi Leja, while Bill and I continued along the Byzantine way and soon reached the junction with Abbas Pasha's path. We turned right and descended Mount Sinai's slope following the same route that we had ascended the previous day. The meeting of the two paths is about twenty minutes' walk from the defile that had been blasted and the steps. The mountain scenery was spectacular. Above us was the brownish massif of Mount Sinai. In the middle distance and below us to the right the small white chapel at the peak of Jebel Moneijat stood out. The broad valley at the foot of Jebel Musa was also visible. It was the size of this valley that convinced the nineteenth-century travelers of the identification of Jebel Musa as Mount Sinai, for it seemed to them large enough for the Israelite camp at the giving of the law.

The descent was surprisingly steep, and I realized that my fatigue of the previous day had been justified. Toward evening, we reached the monastery and found the hostel more deserted than it had been on Saturday night, although there were still some tourists, and the vehicle from Pat's Desert Tours of Cairo that I had observed earlier was still there. Bill was not feeling well—we had been severely sunburned the previous day, but an evening's rest had restored him—my guess was that he had also become somewhat dehydrated. Bill and I made dinner and ate. Then while he rested, I went out to walk around the grounds to warm up.

While out I encountered a strange sight: a large group of German tourists who had come in a bus cross-country from Europe. They did not stay in the hostel because the bus was fitted with three stories of bunks in the rear where they slept, while in its front half there was a sitting area for about twenty people. In the dusk I caught sight of them with a Roman Catholic priest celebrating mass on the lawn in front of the main gate of the monastery. I saw them again two days later, for they had stayed the night and were still touring the area. They had broken out tables and chairs and had set up for breakfast in the sun before the main gate of the monastery. A sensible way to travel, I thought, if one had good companions. However, the idea of setting up tables and chairs unprotected in the desert sun on a warm morning (and the day was warm) would occur only to Europeans, and the scene struck me as rather bizarre.

On the day we arrived and on the day we left, we observed desert tour vehicles from Neot Hakikar, the successful Israeli company that offered such expeditions. These are approved tourist vehicles, so the Egyptians allowed them to come to the monastery. We had seen them also on our earlier visit.

The number of people in the hostel changed from day to day, depending on the planes and the surface vehicles that arrived. Still, it was nothing like the populous Israeli tours that had visited the field school in previous times. On the day we arrived, a plane had also come in from Cairo, and on that Saturday night the monastery hostel was quite full. We were the only Israelis staying over, but there were Egyptians, French, Germans, and a few Americans. The bedouin responsible cooked food for them in the kitchen, although we ate our own supplies in the room. The water, which comes by syphon from Wadi Leja, was quite cold, and in the bathrooms there was no warm water. We had to do without the luxury of the hot showers we had enjoyed in Avner Goren's quarters on previous trips.

The whole time that we were at the monastery, except for the soldiers on Jebel Musa, we saw no Egyptian military or police. The feeling of being almost strangers in a familiar place, a sort of déjà vu with a difference, was acute.

Monday, 25 February 1980

Our plan for Monday was simple. Michal had arranged for Father Sophronius, a friend of hers, to show us around the monastery, where we would search for inscriptions that previous scholars had noted. We rose quite late again, about 8:00, and took a leisurely breakfast. The monastery opened to visitors only at about 9:30. We walked up and were given a most detailed tour of the famous site. Its central features are the burning bush (Exod 3:2-4) and the relics of Saint Catherine. The monastery has been described many times. In the years 1956–1965 two universities, Princeton and Michigan, undertook expeditions, and the resulting book presents the monastery in wonderful photographs.[5] We visited certain parts of the complex of buildings not normally visited by tourists. The old laundry with its ovens for heating water and enormous copper bowls was one. Another was

---

5. George H. Forsyth and Kurt Weitzmann, *The Monastery of Saint Catherine at Mount Sinai: The Church and Fortress of Justinian* (Ann Arbor: University of Michigan Press, 1973).

5. THE FOURTH EXPEDITION, 23–25 FEBRUARY 1980

the former refectory, with Crusader coats-of-arms in the stone over the entrance and magnificent carved wooden tables.

When we arrived, Father Dionysus, the oeconomus in charge of the financial affairs of the monastery, invited us up to his office. He offered us coffee, which was served by a bedouin, and chatted with us while we paid for our lodgings. Michal was to be a guest of the monastery, while we paid our $7 per night. On the wall of his room were all the keys of the monastery storerooms and a plan of them in Greek. Father Dionysus had made this plan some years before during a previous stint as oeconomus. He was quite proud of it and pleased at the interest we took in it. Bill spent time puzzling out the Modern Greek of the plan. We talked with Father Dionysus in English, while Michal talked with him in Arabic.

Father Sophronius had been at Saint Catherine's, he told us, for thirty-four years. A lively man, he was given to excitement and shouting, and after I met him I realized that it was he who had shouted so energetically at our camel driver that first morning. He was a delightful and well-informed guide. While we waited for him, Bill and I examined the famous lift that had provided the sole access to the monastery in troubled times. It had been restored with new wooden poles and ropes, and today it serves for the elevation of large objects and burdens that could not otherwise be introduced into the monastery. The platform juts out of the wall above the door through which the tourists enter the monastery. A remarkable view from one corner of the walls is highlighted by a much ornamented bell that Father Sophronius assured us was made in Odessa a hundred years ago. It is unclear whether this is one of the nine bells donated by Czar Alexander II of Russia (1855–1881).

We also examined the wells. The identification of Miriam's Well is based on a tradition common to Judaism, Christianity, and Islam. In addition to Miriam's Well, there were two other wells in the monastery, but these sources of water had become contaminated by sewage (a new sewer system was to be installed). A siphon in a black plastic pipe now brought water from the springs of Wadi Leja. Bedouin children occasionally punctured it, producing a great geyser of water. This explains the geyser that I had observed on a previous visit. The siphon ran around the base of Jebel Safsafa and was under considerable pressure. This problem with the water supply rendered the monastery vulnerable, for there was no independent system of cisterns for the storage of drinking water.

This same Father Sophronius was the one who discovered the walled-up room of manuscripts in the aftermath of a fire in 1975. These manuscripts included the missing pages of the famous Codex Sinaiticus, a fourth-century master codex of the Greek Bible. There are Greek manuscripts, of course, and Christian Arabic, Syriac, and Georgian, as well as the only written samples of the language of the Christian Caucasian Albanians. I have thought much about why the monks are so wary of outsiders, particularly as far as their treasures are concerned. Some people lay the blame on Tischendorf, the German scholar of the nineteenth century who made off with the Codex Sinaiticus, one of the great manuscripts of the Greek Bible. He left, I recall from my reading, in the famous lift. The monks display a photocopy and translation of a letter he left there in which he undertook to return the book. His story is different, that he saved it from destruction. In any case, it was sold to the czar of Russia and eventually, after the Bolshevik Revolution, purchased by the British Museum, where it rests to this day. This is an example of the acquisitiveness of nineteenth-century scholars who "transferred" many manuscripts from the Near East to the great museums and libraries of Europe.

It is a moot question in my mind whether the Tischendorf affair is more than an excuse for today's monks' reluctance to publicize their holdings. It is difficult to gain access to long-known manuscripts and the monastery's extremely important collection of icons. I find it quite understandable that this material is not shown to the crowds of tourists, for it deteriorates under display conditions and would also pose major security challenges. The reserved attitude toward scholars is, however, less readily comprehensible.

We were excited when we identified three Armenian inscriptions on the church doors. This changed our view of things somewhat. The Armenian and Greek churches split in 451 CE at an ecumenical council over theological issues. Each regards the other as heretical. Consequently, we had thought that Armenian pilgrims were unlikely to have had anything to do with the Greek Saint Catherine's Monastery. However, both the monastery's holding of at least one Armenian manuscript and now the three inscriptions of the church door indicated that Armenians did have contact with the monastery. We examined both sides of all four wooden doors as carefully as we could. The light was poor and access was difficult. On that day we found only these three Armenian inscriptions. Then we returned to the hostel for lunch and some rest. Bill was still feeling a bit under the weather, so he stayed in and relaxed. I joined Michal in the mid-afternoon for a walk over to the bedouin village. She visited some friends there and tried to find out whether she could secure permission to stay in the Sinai until the end on the week. We were to fly back to Jerusalem on the noon plane the next day.

I set out to return to the monastery from the bedouin village as it grew dark. Along the way I examined some rocks with Nabatean inscriptions in Wadi el-Deir that I had noted on our previous visits. I walked into a magnificent sunset. Ahead of me Wadi el-Deir and the monastery were already in shadow. Jebel Moneijat and Jethro's Tomb, beyond the monastery, still glittered in the sun, as did the peaks of Jebel Safsafa. By the time I reached the monastery, all was in shadow except the very highest peaks.

I found Bill much improved by his rest, and we had a long discussion of the inscriptions we had found and of the material inside the church. Our intention had been to take a walk to some of the surrounding areas the next morning, but it seemed to us as we talked over the find that we must return to the church and examine the doors again with the aid of the flashlight that I had brought. This proved to be a fortunate decision. In the first place, we found another tiny inscription. Second, we could confirm our readings and measurements of the first three inscriptions. Since we were not allowed to take photos, I was dependent on my notes and records. Strangely enough, only when I got home did I connect one of the inscriptions with an inscription that I had found in Wadi Mukattab. The writing was identical and most distinctive. The excitement and pressure of the work at Saint Catherine's did not leave me time or energy for such identifications.

Tuesday, 26 February 1980

On Monday evening I felt unwell with what seemed like a touch of flu. I went to bed early and rested; by morning I had quite recovered. On Tuesday morning we rose about 8:00, packed and sorted the gear, and at 9:00 we attempted to enter the monastery, although it was closed until 9:30. When we appeared at that time, the level area under the side entrance was already filling up with the numerous one-day tourists. The monks were late opening up the side door, and these tourists became more and more impatient. One of them spent a long time pounding on the door to no avail. Only at about 10:00 did the monks open up.

While Bill and I were off at the monastery in the morning, Michal sorted the food, taking with our blessing those provisions she thought she might need during the rest of her stay in the Sinai. She intended to be off in the mountains visiting friends in various places. Tuesday is a tourist day, and the crowds started to flow up to the monastery. The priest there was most helpful to us, however, in our examination of the doors. When we finished, we bought some cards and slides and a rather wonderful map of the monastery dated 1979 (fig. 7). Then we set off by foot for the outer gate of the monastery. We knew that the Arkia plane had arrived, since the group of tourists from the plane was already at the monastery.

We went to the airport, which we reached by bus from the main gate of the monastery. There we went through the formalities of redeeming our passports. Michal managed to arrange a permit for an extended stay in the area and left us there. We flew smoothly to Eilat airport, where we changed planes for Jerusalem. All went as planned, and late that afternoon I arrived home. On the way, I had the taxi stop by the photographer, and I left off the film for developing and printing. The discoveries of this expedition were major: we had enlarged the corpus of Armenian inscriptions by about thirty, as well as finding what seemed to be two Georgian ones.

After my return to Jerusalem, I consulted Archbishop Norayr Bogharian at the Armenian Patriarchate. He had published the text of the fifteenth-century inscriptions we had photographed on the peak of Mount Sinai, but he was not familiar with the others. At once I set about trying to arrange for funds to cover the expenses of achieving the two goals that were still ahead of me: one was to examine the Wadi Zalaqa area of eastern Sinai and to complete the survey of Wadi Ḥajjaj; the other was to get professional photographs of the inscriptions in Wadi Ḥajjaj. With political conditions changing almost daily, it was essential that I complete the work as quickly as possible.

* * * *

Some time after my return, I visited the library of the Institute of Archaeology of the Hebrew University. There I carefully examined the photographs in Weizmann and Forsythe's magnificent collection of photographs of Saint Catherine's Monastery.[6] Knowing where to look, I was able to locate certain of the inscriptions on the wooden doors of the church.

The weeks after my return home were spent on matters other than the Sinai. I took the time to write up this diary and to prepare the preliminary edition of the inscriptions we had found. I was unable, however, to advance arrangements for my next visit. The problem was chiefly financial.

---

6. Forsyth and Weitzmann, *The Monastery of Saint Catherine*.

5. THE FOURTH EXPEDITION, 23–25 FEBRUARY 1980

Avner Goren was more than willing to help, but his budget had run out. Even though the new financial year had started, his budget was not yet approved. So my first plan, to go in early May, fell through. At the same time, I eagerly awaited the results of a meeting Avner was to have on 2 June to try to free up his budget. I decided to go to Wadi Zalaqa at the end of June regardless.

On 3 June I telephoned Avner Goren. The budget for the jeep had come through, he told me. I telephoned Uzi in Eilat, and we made plans to go down to the Sinai, to Wadi Zalaqa, at the end of the month.

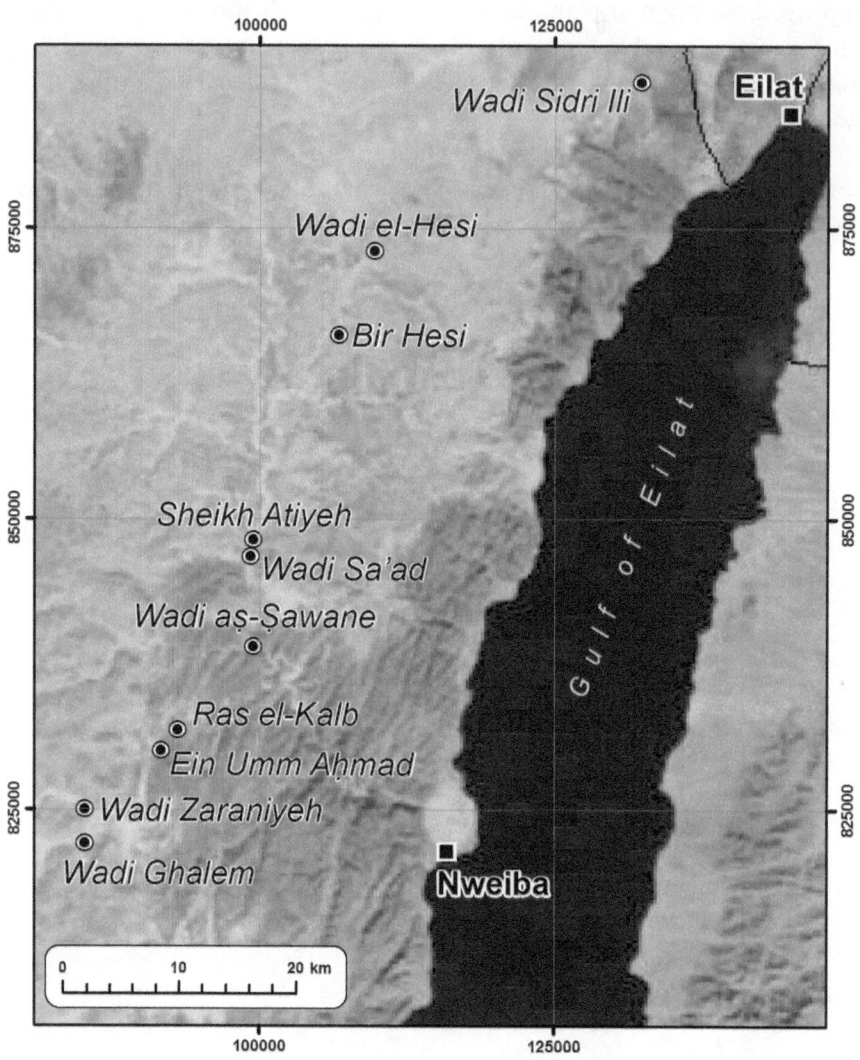

Map 5. Eilat to Wadi Zarniyeh

6
THE FIFTH EXPEDITION
14–18 JULY 1980

I set out on this final expedition with a plan of achieving two different aims. The first was to take a professional photographer to Wadi Ḥajjaj to photograph the Armenian inscriptions that we had found at that site. I was preparing the final publication of the Sinai Armenian inscriptions and hoped that a professional might get better photographs than Uzi and I had taken.[1] This aim fitted in admirably with the often-deferred plan to complete the survey of the Wadi Ḥajjaj and ʿEin Ḥudra areas. Since the finds in that area were so remarkable, I thought that it should be surveyed systematically once more. The second aim was to follow up the report of an Armenian inscription in the area of Wadi Zalaqa. An inscription in Wadi Zalaqa would be significant not just in itself but also because it might open discussion of this route as a possible major pilgrim path through eastern Sinai.

I should explain that, as I tried to make sense of our finds so far, my interests had broadened. When I started these Sinai adventures, I was keen to look for Armenian inscriptions. Now, in order to understand the distribution of the Armenian inscriptions, I also sought to find out as much as I could about the human traffic, particularly pilgrim traffic, on the desert routes, in order to gain insight into who went where, when, and, if possible, why.

The difficulty of understanding the eastern Sinai became much more worrisome to me as my investigations progressed during the months preceding this expedition. The problem was this: ancient pilgrim reports all

---

1. Michael E. Stone, *The Armenian Inscriptions from the Sinai with Appendixes on the Georgian and Latin Inscriptions by Michel van Esbroeck and William Adler*, Harvard Armenian Texts and Studies 6 (Cambridge: Harvard University Press, 1982).

refer to the western Sinai route through Wadi Mukattab and Wadi Feiran, with the exception of two sixth-century writers. One writer stated that from Eilat (ancient Aila) to Mount Sinai was a journey of eight days. The other said that travel from Elusa (Halutza), an important city in the Negev, until one enters the desert takes seven or eight days, then an additional eight days in the desert to Mount Sinai. So, taking these reports as a point of departure, I tried to work out the routes traveled by the pilgrims from Elusa and from Eilat. I sought to formulate hypotheses that I could verify during the course of this last expedition.

I concluded that there were three possible routes from Elusa to Saint Catherine's. The westernmost one ran through Naḫl, traversed the Tih plateau, then descended through one of the passes over the Tih, such as Naqb Rakna, which we had examined. This was the way Felix Fabri had traveled. This route then joined the way that ran from Egypt, through the great valleys of western Sinai. We had traversed this very route in our expedition to Naqb Rakna. The other two routes from Elusa crossed eastern Sinai. One of them traveled down Wadi el-Ḥesi, a broad valley that runs north to south, then bears southwest along Wadi Zalaqa as far as Ras Zalaqa (Ras means "head" in Arabic), which is about 40 kilometers north of Saint Catherine's monastery. This route is easy and short.

From the end of Wadi el-Ḥesi it was also possible, instead of bearing southwest along Wadi Zalaqa, to bear southeast for a short distance along Wadi Watir and thus to reach 'Ein Fortaga and the complex of wadis of which Wadi Ḥajjaj is a part. A variant of this route was to travel down the coast and then turn inland along Wadi Watir to 'Ein Fortaga and from there through Wadi Ḥajjaj or other closely related valleys and thence through one of a number of possible routes to Mount Sinai. This coastal route, although Burckhardt traveled it, was not likely to have been much used, for in some places the mountains reached down to the sea, making passage difficult.

Uzi had visited Wadi Zalaqa previously. As well as many rock drawings in the area at the head of the wadi, he had noted Nabatean and Greek inscriptions. Shauly, Avner Goren's assistant, had told me of an inscription there "in your letters," meaning either Armenian or Georgian. So there was good reason to go there, but I was uncertain whether it would be possible, as the Israeli withdrawal from the Sinai was then underway. Avner Goren told me that most of the area with the inscriptions was still under Israeli control. Naturally, it would be ideal if I could examine the area myself, particularly since Armenian inscriptions were often difficult

6. THE FIFTH EXPEDITION, 14–18 JULY 1980

to see because they were small in size and I had developed skill in spotting and identifying them.

The preparations for this expedition were long and arduous. I had made application to various foundations for funds, since the costs of photography, together with the jeep and other expenses, came to a considerable sum. I wanted to finish all the fieldwork before I left for a year in the Netherlands in August 1980. The political situation was so fluid that, if I waited a year, it might prove impossible for me to get to this area.

My application to the various Armenian foundations had been turned down, since the project was rather out of their usual line of activity. Eventually my work was made possible by a grant from the Harvard Semitic Museum, made available through the good offices of my friend and teacher, Frank Cross, who was a distinguished epigrapher, although not of Armenian. He had followed our Sinai work from the beginning and came to our rescue at this crucial juncture. In addition, the Institute of Jewish Studies at the Hebrew University was generous enough to make me a grant toward the photographic expenses. In late May I also received support from a source in Australia. These sums made the work possible and turned out to be particularly timely. Although Avner Goren had promised me the use of a jeep, this never happened. We postponed the trip to Wadi Zalaqa twice, but still the jeep did not materialize. Then Avner had to leave for a month's visit to Greece, and I had to make my own arrangements. In these circumstances, the availability of funds was crucial. In desperation, I turned to Uzi's boss in the Israel Antiquities Authority, who agreed to bend the rules and let me use his vehicle, as long as I paid all the expenses.

Before returning to Wadi Hajjaj with Zev Radovan, an exceptionally gifted photographer who had done a lot of archaeological work, I reviewed all the photos taken so far from the Wadi Hajjaj region. Zev, too, had examined all my photos carefully. We decided to make a full set of new photos on the spot and then to select the very best of his and mine for eventual publication. In the course of examining the photos, particularly of Rock III at Wadi Hajjaj, I had noted a number of points at which I thought there might be Armenian inscriptions I had not detected.

This was so in spite of the fact that I had already spent four full days examining these rocks. I have observed before that the nature of the stone and the delicacy with which the inscriptions are incised makes them appear and disappear in the changing light of the different hours of the day and different seasons of the year (fig. 21).

A subsidiary aim of our visit to Wadi Ḥajjaj was to examine one or two wadis in the area. We had received several reports of inscriptions, particularly in Wadi Rum, which we had tried to enter on a previous trip, unsuccessfully.[2]

Monday, 14 July 1980

We departed Jerusalem on the 7:30 AM plane. I was accompanied by Zev and my daughter Aurit, who was coming for the experience. When we reached Eilat, it was quite hot. There was a heat wave during all the time we were in the Sinai. Uzi, with his daughter Yael, picked us up in the jeep at the airport. The mountains of Edom to the east in the Kingdom of Jordan were hazy and unclear, but the mountains to the west of Eilat were particularly sharply visible. Mary, a member of Uzi's team, joined us, bringing five loaves of bread and other provisions; we fueled up the jeep and set off about 9:30. The odometer of the jeep showed 25,483 kilometers when we started; when we completed our expedition five days later, we had traveled 800 kilometers, which is a great deal for predominantly desert travel.

The run down to Wadi Ḥajjaj was as beautiful as always, and we stopped briefly at the Coral Island and the Fjord, two of the prime scenic sites on the route. Aurit and Yael enjoyed the views. At Nweiba, we looked for the representative of the Nature Preserves Authority; we wanted a note from him to Jum'a, the bedouin watchman at Wadi Ḥajjaj, so that he would let us work peacefully. We got the note, and when we arrived and handed it to Jum'a, he looked at it respectfully, even though it was in Hebrew. I am sure he did not read Hebrew and am by no means certain that he read Arabic. However, the note was on the proper stationery, and he let us work peacefully and comfortably during our stay there.

By 11:00 AM the temperature was 37 degrees Celsius (98 Fahrenheit). We were on the road from Nweiba to Wadi Ḥajjaj and watched the jeep warm up on the long ascent. The heat indicator rose steadily. We took the air temperature at the bottom and at the top of the ascent, expecting to find up to six degrees difference (cooler at the top), which is usual. In fact, that day only a couple of degrees separated them. Several days later I made the ascent again, and that time I did observe the usual difference of temperature.

---

2. See pages 56–57 above.

6. THE FIFTH EXPEDITION, 14–18 JULY 1980

Roughly 2 kilometers east of Wadi Ḥajjaj we observed rock drawings on the rocks on the north side of the road. I carefully surveyed these when we revisited the area three days later.

The work at Wadi Ḥajjaj was hard and not very promising. I located the Armenian inscriptions, and Zev photographed them. Many were familiar, but during the whole process of photography I discovered new ones in that area. We ate our lunch and dinner on the site and slept there as well. Having Uzi's jeep made a good deal of difference, since he had fitted it with a number of special adaptations for the desert, many of which he had made himself. One was a tarpaulin attached to the side of the jeep's roof. This formed a good shade tent when unrolled from the side of the jeep and supported by two poles. At night, when the wind came up, the same tarpaulin, weighted down with stones, made an excellent windbreak.

In the late afternoon we took the children to see the *nawamis*, the beehive tombs, while we were waiting for the light to change. The two girls seemed to enjoy their time in the desert very much, in spite of the quite difficult physical conditions. Our food was particularly good this trip, since Mary took charge of it and showed herself to be an excellent field cook. Nevertheless, it was, as usual, not really haute cuisine.

Tuesday, 15 July 1980

The next day we rose at 5:00 AM and set out from our camping place by 5:30 to enable Zev to take as many photographs as possible in the dawn light. Once again I discovered new Armenian inscriptions as we worked together. By 7:30 the thermometer read 28 degrees Celsius (82 Fahrenheit); it was summer, after all. We worked until 8:30, when we stopped for breakfast. During the work, bedouin children and tourist groups accompanied us as well. A final set of photos of Rock III (see fig. 21) concluded our work, and I made a last discovery: two more Armenian inscriptions. Then at 9:35 we set off to Wadi Rum.

Wadi Rum is one of a series of intersecting wadis around 'Ein Ḥudra. It runs between Wadi Ḥudra and an area to the west of Wadi Ḥajjaj; we had tried to enter it on a previous occasion.[3] At that time Fatḥi had feared that his jeep would become mired in the sand dune at its entrance, a baseless fear, as we soon found out. It is conceivable that travelers having reached

---

3. See pages 57–58 above.

Fig. 21. Goats and inscriptions on Rock III, Wadi Ḥajjaj

'Ein Fortaga, either via the coast road or via Wadi el-Ḥesi and Wadi Watir, might have traveled on by Wadi Ghazaleh and Wadi Rum and exited at the sand dune. This would have put them in an excellent position for easy travel toward Jebel Musa via Wadi Mara.

First we looked at the *hadbes*, the great sandstone monoliths near the head of the wadi, where we found some fairly recently incised crosses and many rock drawings. We photographed these, then entered Wadi Rum.

Within the wadi the wild broken rocks—brown with red tints to them—created a powerful vista. They were all sandstone, which is plentiful in this area. About 1.5 kilometers into the wadi we came across a group of *hadbes* with Nabatean inscriptions. There was a Nabatean holy site there, with two standing stones, separated by a low stone in the middle. They were so aligned that worshipers prostrating themselves and looking over the stones would see the impressive mountain directly ahead. The earlier wild, red, broken cliffs gave way to majestic crags rising up from the white sand underfoot. *Hadbes* with drawings continued to occur for another 2 kilometers, and then these gave way to grey granite. A tall thin finger of rock stood isolated in the wadi floor; it is one of the more remarkable features of Wadi Rum. After another kilometer or so, we were forced to stop about 700 meters from the junction with Wadi Ḥudra, since the wadi was too narrow to pass. So we retraced our path, the return trip up the wadi taking only ten minutes. We passed rocks with Nabatean drawings and another standing stone, but there were no Christian monuments in the wadi, which disappointed us. Again we had been led astray by oral reports: nonexperts tend to confuse rock drawings with inscriptions.

When we approached the notorious sand dune, Uzi put the jeep into gear and setting off at great speed succeeded in getting two-thirds of the way up the incline. Then the jeep bogged down in the soft sand. The passengers got out, and Uzi backed the vehicle down a bit, then set off energetically—and successfully—for the top of the dune. We passengers climbed this last section of the ascent on foot and remounted the jeep at the top. By now the temperature had risen yet higher.

From Wadi Rum we returned to the track in Wadi Ḥajjaj, then proceeded east as far as the junction of Wadi Ghazaleh. Here we turned off with the purpose of following this wadi to the point where it joined Wadi Ḥudra and then returning along Wadi Ḥudra as far as the spring of ʿEin Ḥudra. We had traveled the Wadi Ghazaleh before, and the way was sandy and particularly draining on fuel. Just before ʿEin Ḥudra we saw a group of people camped in the shade of a cliff in the heat of the day. It turned out to be a Danish man with his French wife and two children, two bedouin, and some camels. They were guiding a group of four Belgian tourists for a week of camel travel. The Danish family had adopted a bedouin way of life. They had unloaded their camels, and there were water skins of various sizes scattered around. As we arrived the woman was chewing away at a rather large piece of dried fish.[4] The children with their straw blond hair looked strange in bedouin clothing, yet the scene had the romance of desert travel to it. The man described two *hadbes* nearby, close to the White Canyon, that seemed worth examining. It was too late for us to verify the report that day, but we decided to do so after we visited Wadi Zalaqa.

At this juncture, as I regarded this group of people, the possibility occurred to me that pilgrims may have stopped in the middle of the day for a rest and used that time to write graffiti. Later I learned from reading travel narratives that this idea, though a little romantic, was quite unrealistic. The pilgrim reports clearly indicate that, once the camels were loaded

---

4. John Lewis Burckhardt describes the bedouin method of preparing this fish in *Travels in Syria and the Holy Land* (London: Murray, 1822), 504.

Fig. 22. 'Ein Ḥudra

in the morning, they moved on without stopping until they unloaded for the night. The pilgrims used to start out early when possible and to make camp before dark. Quite often the travelers themselves rode donkeys while camels carried their baggage. Those on donkeys could stop and did so in some instances.[5] The midday camel stop, however, was a figment of my imagination.

After this encounter, we drove on to 'Ein Ḥudra (figs. 22–23). By the time we arrived there, we were down to the last dregs of fuel in the jeep's tank, so we filled up with the reserve gasoline we had with us. At 'Ein Ḥudra the bedouin have built a sort of water trough, and an aqueduct from the spring brings water to it. We filled our spare water containers from this trough. Where the water overflows the trough, fine green grass the color you see on a lawn-bowling green has sprouted, which looks strange in the heart of the desert. However, in the Sinai, wherever there is water, there is vegetation. At 'Ein Ḥudra there is another walled bedouin garden with numerous date palms and other trees. We made a brief survey of the area for inscriptions but found nothing.

---

5. See page 132 above.

6. THE FIFTH EXPEDITION, 14–18 JULY 1980

The visit to 'Ein Ḥudra was important, however, for this water source must have formed the first and primary attraction that brought the pilgrims to the area of Wadi Ḥajjaj. In ancient times one or possibly two ascents were used from 'Ein Ḥudra to the Wadi Ḥajjaj area. The bedouin made the present pass, from the northern point of Wadi Ḥajjaj, several generations ago. One of the local men knew that his grandfather had contributed to that work.

As said before, Wadi Ḥajjaj is not the only wadi easily accessible from 'Ein Ḥudra, and it also provides ready access to the roads leading toward Jebel Musa. So the question of why the inscriptions were limited to Wadi Ḥajjaj continued to haunt us.

We completed our visit at 'Ein Ḥudra at 1:15 PM. On the thermometer the temperature in the shade was now just over 40 degrees Celsius (104 Fahrenheit). The heat was palpable; you felt it as though it were an object. The jeep started to heat up, with the needle on its dial just below the boiling point. We retraced our steps along Wadi Ḥudra to Wadi Ghazaleh and then to 'Ein Fortaga. The bed of the wadi changed from flat sand to gravel. The sandstone yielded to granite cliffs, gray in color with a greenish tint in places. On the way we saw scattered acacia trees and some bedouin

Fig. 23. Bedouin men near 'Ein Ḥudra

encampments. The bedouin at 'Ein Ḥudra belong to the Muzeineh tribe, while 'Ein Fortaga is in the territory of the Tarabin. There was once great enmity between these two tribes, but this has muted in recent years.

Two bedouin women hailed us and asked for food. The one who talked with us showed great interest in Yael; she was veiled and barefooted, and we gave her half a loaf of bread. With transparent guile she then asked, "What do you put on the bread?" But we could not help her any more.

'Ein Fortaga is a site we had already visited. As a result of the drought in the Sinai, the water level in the oasis had dropped below the level we had seen fifteen months earlier. The pool by which Uzi, Tom, and I had drunk coffee was now completely dry. Two days later we approached the same oasis from the west, through Wadi Watir. Uzi remarked that not very many years ago one traveled Wadi Watir in running water from a point about 8 kilometers north of the oasis of 'Ein Fortaga. Now it was dry for most of its length, and all that remained of the once-generous flow were some pools near the junction of the wadis. There was a good amount of vegetation, however, and we saw the intense green of the Colocynth (the bitter apple or vine of Sodom), which is used in homeopathic medicine. Felix Fabri relates how at one oasis the members of his group ignored the warnings of their guide and eagerly fell upon this attractive-looking fruit. They were unpleasantly surprised by its astringent, bitter taste.[6]

Some palm trees had partly died and were lying dry along the side of the wadi, which bore clear signs of earlier years' generous water flows. However, closer to the spring itself the palms were green and colorful. This oasis is impressive, as I have already remarked, because it is located in a fairly narrow wadi between steep, stark granite cliffs. Alas, this most remarkable site bore no inscriptions.

We did not delay at 'Ein Fortaga, although I watched carefully all through this area for inscriptions. Some distance past it we encountered two French women stranded by a car, which they and a companion had tried to drive through Wadi Watir to 'Ein Fortaga. They had knocked a hole in one of the leads of their automatic transmission, which had lost its fluid. We gave them some water; they were unwilling to have us move their car aside. Farther on we came across their companion. He had apparently

---

6. H. F. M. Prescott, *Once to Sinai: The Further Pilgrimage of Friar Felix Fabri* (New York: Macmillan, 1958), 54.

6. THE FIFTH EXPEDITION, 14–18 JULY 1980

gone to summon some bedouin with a jeep to tow them. The jeep, however, had run out of gasoline, so he and one of the bedouin had walked to the car, siphoned some gasoline out of its tank, and were proceeding on foot back to the jeep. We gave them a ride, and apparently they extricated themselves for, when we passed through again two days later, the only sign of the incident was the stain of the transmission fluid on the path. This reminded me of a similar experience on a previous visit to 'Ein Fortaga, when we had helped a man get a car out of the sand. Except for the Wadi Sa'al–Wadi Mara road, not much can be traversed in the Sinai without a high-profile, four-wheel-drive vehicle.

When we arrived at Nweiba, we fueled up the jeep. Since we had time, we drove down to the beach, lunched there, and took a swim. The jeep carried us out on the long, sandy promontory of Nweiba, which had become a well-known camping and recreation site. There were quite a number of people there, particularly sunbathers in various states of undress, and it seemed quite crowded after the desert emptiness. By going a good distance out, we found a spot that was deserted enough for our taste. We swam in the lukewarm water; it was low tide, and the lagoon behind the reef was shallow. Not having snorkeling gear, I could not see much of the fish and coral that abounded, and there are other places on the coast much better for snorkeling than Nweiba. It was refreshing, however, and the two girls particularly enjoyed it.

We had lunch by the jeep there, and we could feel the difference between the air on the beach and that of the dry desert inland. An even more delightful contrast with dry desert heat was the ice cream that we had bought at the local gas station. We were hot, dusty, and rather dehydrated, so to come to Nweiba and eat ice cream was a delightful experience. I do not think that I have ever eaten ice cream that tasted so good.

After lunch, taken in the shade of the tarpaulin side of the jeep, we set out northward to Eilat. We needed to be there in time for a 6:00 plane because the photographer Zev and Aurit were flying back to Jerusalem. We still had one stop en route, however, a site called Bir Sweir. This water source on the coast was an obvious stopping point for pilgrims coming south from Eilat on the coastal route. There is a well-known group of inscriptions, not at the well itself, which is to the east of the road, but at the mouth of the wadi to the west.

A number of tumbled sandstone rocks form a set of crannies and caves at the mouth of Wadi Sweir. The drawings that covered many of the rocks were of ordinary character, but some of them had a patina almost identical with the rock, perhaps a sign of considerable age.[7] There are many crosses on the rocks in different styles and shapes, some of them elegant in style and execution. Certain rocks had as many as a dozen crosses, and the total came to well over fifty. The rocks also bore Greek inscriptions. They were about 400 meters inland from the road, while the well itself was several hundred meters on the other side of the road. In other words, the Bir Sweir inscriptions conformed to the pattern observed elsewhere: they were at some distance from the water source, in this case about 600 meters. I have remarked previously on the reasons usually given for sleeping at some distance from water sources. Here the shelter of the rocks may also have been a secondary contributing factor.

Another matter of this sort should be discussed at this point. We frequently found the inscriptions to be located on the eastern and northern faces of rocks or wadis. This was not always the case, but it occurred often enough to raise questions. It seems probable that pilgrims wrote the graffiti at times when they were resting from their journeys.

Flinders Petrie, the great Egyptologist, says of desert travel, "We rested from 12.30 to 1.40, but the camels went on till 4.45."[8] Indeed, he relates, the cameleers wished to stop at 2:15, but he insisted on pushing on. The comments of travelers such as Leonardo Frescobaldi (1384) give the same impression. According to Felix Fabri, the camel trains started out early in the morning, even before dawn. They traveled continuously until mid-afternoon, when the camels stopped, and camp was set up. Fabri's report is particularly important, for his group, like most pilgrims, knew no Arabic and nothing of the desert ways. Petrie, on the other hand, had lived in the Middle East for decades when he wrote. Avner Goren and others with whom I discussed this matter knew nothing of this custom, but then modern conditions are quite different from those of the medieval pilgrims.[9] If the picture Felix Fabri gives is correct, and Petrie's observations corroborate it, then the camping pilgrims would naturally have sought out the northern and eastern faces of the rocks and cliffs, for these were shaded in the afternoon hours. This might be a partial explanation

---

7. The difficulty of dating by patina is that it is created by chemical reaction between dampness deep in the rocks and the material of the surface rock. The rate of this reaction is governed as much by exposure and wind as by the amount of time passed.

8. W. M. Flinders Petrie, *Researches in Sinai* (New York: Dutton, 1906), 10.

9. Indeed, the camels who bear burdens have certain stages, beyond which they will not go, but rest at the end of them.

6. THE FIFTH EXPEDITION, 14–18 JULY 1980

at least for the siting of the inscriptions predominantly on these sides of the rocks.

In any case, the importance of the Bir Sweir inscriptions is that they confirmed the coastal route that we had anticipated. This is particularly significant when we bear in mind that the modern travelers who used this route stress the fact that they did not regard it as a major thoroughfare. We visited the site at about 4:45 in the afternoon and reached Eilat soon after. I saw Aurit and Zev safely onto the plane, and we returned to Uzi's home in Eilat, where we spent the night.

Wednesday, 16 July 1980

As so often happens, our departure in the morning was delayed. We were quite a substantial party. There were, in addition to Uzi and me, four other people. One was Mary of Uzi's staff, who had been to Wadi Ḥajjaj; she stayed with us for two of the next three days. With her was her boyfriend, Eyal, a graduate student in physical education who was taking some time off from his studies and working in the Eilat area. Another couple, Anat and Tal, joined us; they used us as transport to a particularly lovely oasis where they wanted to spend a couple of days.

Uzi went off to take Yael to the airport and to get the jeep fixed. It had developed an oil leak from the rear axle. With his staff, I spent the time in the flat, making notes of the results of the Wadi Ḥajjaj expedition and doing some preliminary planning for the coming days. We hoped to advance one step further in our study of the pilgrim routes in eastern Sinai by examining the routes through the eastern part of the peninsula.

Uzi had shown me at his home a handsome plaque he had received as a gift from the American general in charge of the building of the airfield (now mainly civilian) known as Uvda Airport, about 60 kilometers north of Eilat. Uzi had done all he could to preserve and record as much as possible of the archaeological evidence of the area being cleared and leveled for the airfield. I had talked with him on the phone at the height of this activity; it had been very intensive. The archaeological sites there were not dramatic and so were easily missed in the course of construction. Therefore, Uzi had given the army engineers a hard time, or as hard a time as he could. His efforts had been partly successful, and much unnecessary destruction had been avoided. The plaque was an expression of respect for Uzi's work. On it were Indian arrow heads, some of considerable age, and a dedication from the general.

It was nearly 10:00 by the time we departed. Mary and her friends had completed most of the preparations and had loaded the jeep. We drove westward from Eilat on the paved road for about 5 kilometers, then turned off on the way that leads to the Canyon of Inscriptions, a place we did not visit. The Canyon of Inscriptions is one of the remarkable epigraphic sites in the Sinai. However, the inscriptions there are not Christian in character, so it was not high on our list of priorities.

It is in an area not far from where we were and is the intersection of major desert travel routes. These were the route from Eilat to Gaza known as Darb Gaza, the route from Eilat to Jebel Musa via Wadi el-Ḥesi and Wadi Zalaqa (the route we were interested in exploring), and the east-west Sinai routes called Darb el-Shawi and Darb el-Ḥajj. Darb el-Ḥajj, or the Road of the Pilgrims, is one of the chief pilgrim routes to Mecca.

We were now traveling over a flat, gravelly area toward a site called Upper Wadi Sidri. Here a series of reddish sandstone rocks form a low cliff 4 or 5 meters high. On these stones are inscriptions in a number of languages: some in Arabic, fifteen or twenty in Nabatean, and perhaps half a dozen in Greek. One badly faded inscription might even have been in Latin, but it was difficult to decide. This site was about 3 kilometers off the road, and we left it at 10:45 to make our way farther south and into Wadi el-Ḥesi.

As we set out from Upper Wadi Sidri, the countryside was quite dramatic, with mountains and craters; after some inspection of the area we continued on our way, bowling south at 60 kilometers an hour over flat ground covered by gray stones and gravel.

The countryside was still wilderness. At a distance of about 15 kilometers into Wadi Sidri III (Upper Wadi Sidri), we were traversing a sandy plain. Suddenly five gazelles appeared to one side of the jeep not far from us. With astounding grace, they leaped across our path and took up a position to the east of our vehicle, several hundred yards away. These creatures are usually timid, and perhaps their daring in this instance shows that hunting has not been extensive here.

We observed rich, green vegetation along a shallow, dry watercourse to our right. The low line of gray shrubs of the plain was backed by a higher row of green bushes, eloquent witness to the rains that had fallen that winter. The region was a broad plain bounded by mountains. The track we were following stood out clearly as a brighter strip on the gray of the plain, in which pebbles alternated with patches of sand. As we proceeded south, we were again struck by the green of the vegetation, in spite of the

6. THE FIFTH EXPEDITION, 14–18 JULY 1980

fact that it was mid-summer. Twelve kilometers farther south, still on the same plain, the mountains began to close in, and we could see them on both sides and ahead of us. The countryside became hillier, and the tributaries of Wadi el-Ḥesi drew closer together; the wadi itself closed in on both sides. The way had been cleared, probably in ancient times. We noted a particularly remarkable cairn, signaling the route, just before a small descent that brought us into the bed of Wadi el-Ḥesi.

A little south of this, at 34 kilometers south of Wadi Sidri III, we came upon an extraordinary site. There were monuments built of stones on both sides of the track. On our right, roughly west, we saw a heap that seemed to be a grave and by it a small shrine with standing stones and an enclosure. On the left of the track, to the east, was a flat stone that bore an Arabic inscription and a faded Greek one. I was unable to make out anything beyond the fact that it was Greek. About 250 meters to the left, that is, to the east of the road and southeast of the first site, we found another three stone circles and a number of flint implements: knives and hammers. These flints were mostly ad hoc tools made on the spot for one-time or brief use (see fig. 24). By then, it was almost exactly noon.

The next point of interest as we continued south was the well-known Bir el-Ḥesi, or Well of Ḥesi. Here there was a large gathering of bedouin flocks. Perhaps a dozen women were gathered around this well, with camels and donkeys as well as the usual sheep and goats. We chatted with the bedouin there, but nothing emerged of interest for our research. By the well were the remains of a building. We made out a courtyard of about 10 meters square and a structure that might have been about 7 meters square. Further stone heaps and Chalcolithic (Copper Age; roughly 4,500–3,500 BCE) sites were visible along the ridge of a hill south of Bir el-Ḥesi.

As we made our way south, the deliberate character of the track we were following became ever clearer. It had been laid along the center, more or less, of the flat area that constituted the bed of Wadi el-Ḥesi. The stones that abound on the surface of the wadi bed had been moved aside to form low heaps along both sides of the track.

About three-quarters of an hour after our observations of the stone heaps north of Bir el-Ḥesi, we saw a Greek inscription. We had traveled another 13 kilometers, and the weather seemed to me a bit cooler than on the previous day. Our thermometer showed 39 degrees Celsius (102 Fahrenheit). Wadi el-Ḥesi was a highway of the desert, still broad and covered with gravel and small stones. The mountains followed us south on both sides of the route; their colors were striking. Large, old acacia trees

Fig. 24. Ad hoc flint tools, Wadi Zalaqa

grew there, and birds flew in clusters across our path. All along the way we could see the distinct road markers. These, together with the ancient sites we found (mainly Chalcolithic), conveyed a feeling of the age-old character of this route.

Ten kilometers farther on we saw a white rock upon which was a modern Arabic inscription. There were numerous tracks alongside the main path and many road markers throughout this part of our journey. Once again, here, even deeper into the wilderness, we were struck by the remarkable amounts of vegetation we observed. At 1:20 PM, having traveled about 60 kilometers south of Wadi Sidri Ili, we had our first flat tire. The change of tire provided the occasion for lunch, so we rigged the tarpaulin roof. It was quite hot by then, and the respite was both deserved and welcome; it is difficult to convey in words the feeling given by the combination of heat and quiet accentuated by the silencing of the jeep's motor. I sensed the emptiness of the area, yet felt that there have been thousands of years of human activity here.

DESERT EMPTINESS
A high peak
mountain craggy
crevices between rocks
hold potsherds once jars

with petroglyphs
stick men
ibex and camels
and flint knives.

MES

Later, while I was in the Netherlands, rereading Petrie's record of his work in Wadi Maghara in western Sinai, I was struck by his remark that the stone monuments and heaps in the wadi beds were evidence that during millennia past there was never much more rain in the Sinai than at the present. These wadis of the Sinai can have sudden, violent floods, but the flow of the waters had not been persistent enough to destroy the heaps of rocks gathered up by humans thousands of years ago. The same also seems to be true of Wadi el-Ḥesi with its stone monuments, cairns, and markers. However, many cairns were so situated as to be above present water levels.

Lunch was welcome and tasty, our usual mayonnaise and cheese to which we added eggs and some salad that we had brought along. We started south again about 2:15. A short distance along the wadi, on the western side, we came across a Muslim holy spot, the tomb called Sheikh 'Atiyah. This is a small building with a domed roof, on a low hill to the side of the path. At the base of the hill is a large acacia tree. A fence, partly in ruins, marks out the edges of the sacred enclosure.

We first sighted Jebel Baraqa 9 kilometers south of our luncheon site. There are three mountains of this name in eastern Sinai, all of them large and distinctive. We had visited the southernmost one on our first trip to Wadi Ḥajjaj over a year before and had found the "Aramaic-style" Nabatean inscriptions at its base. This Jebel Baraqa is a clear breast-shaped mountain with a peak divided in two; it is a remarkable excrescence of rock. On it the unaided eye can trace from afar strata of rock parallel to the ground. The sight of Jebel Baraqa meant that we were approaching the paths leading to the remarkable oasis of 'Ein Umm Aḥmed.

Before we arrived there, however, we came upon the richest site that we had seen since Wadi Sidri III in the north. On the eastern side of the track was a rock face with many drawings on it. It is at the junction of Wadi el-Ḥesi with Wadi Sa'ad. We found drawings, Arabic inscriptions, and one large cross on the north and south sides of this junction. It was an astounding fact, and one that was borne out by our further exploration of Wadi el-Ḥesi, that this highway of the desert, with its cleared track, stone markers, and cairns, had virtually no inscriptions of any type in it. This reinforces the observation that the witness of the inscriptions is positive but never negative. Their presence indicates the presence of travelers, but their absence never *proves* that a route was not used.

The oasis of Bir es-Sawa was almost exactly 15 kilometers south of the point where we had enjoyed lunch. A dozen or more palms surrounded this water source, which is a well with good water. We washed off some of the dirt and felt briefly refreshed. Bir es-Sawa was not quite on the route but about half a kilometer to its west. Some distance off we saw bedouin women with their herds. One of our passengers, who had been there not long before, remarked that the water that had been bitter then was now sweet (shades of Moses in the desert! Exod 15:23–25). There was also a small bedouin cemetery nearby. The place was deserted when we arrived.

The typical stone of the area through which we were now traveling was granite. At 3:20 PM we passed into Wadi Abu Sawane, which runs in a west-southwesterly direction. It is a narrow valley between towering granite cliffs. The terrain was quite rough, and the jeep swayed from side to side like a boat in a turbulent sea. We quickly reached the mountain known as Ras el-Kalb, the Dog's Head. On the saddle of the wadi, between Ras el-Kalb and the mountain opposite, a number of flat rocks lay at the side of the road. These had many inscriptions on them, chiefly in modern Arabic writing. Notable were the large numbers of footprints, many of which had names inside them, something I have not seen elsewhere. This witnesses to, perhaps, the use of the footsteps to indicate where a traveler had gone. The addition of a personal name or a *wasem*, a bedouin tribal

6. THE FIFTH EXPEDITION, 14–18 JULY 1980

mark, confirms this. There were Nabatean inscriptions at this site as well, on the rocks to the south of the way; in addition, about 200 meters distant stood a rock face with some further Nabatean inscriptions. On the return passage the next day, I saw some other writing there, too, in the afternoon sun, but I could not make out what language it was.

The route we were now traveling was impressive and rough. The road ran alongside a gorge of red sandstone cliffs, and on its opposite side we could trace a fairly well built road that had once run there. The Egyptians had demolished it during the Six Day War. At places along this red gorge there had been falls of boulders, but not round ones. Instead, square sandstone boulders were thrown down, and I can only describe the effect with the cliché that they resembled a giant child's building blocks that had tumbled down. I descended from the jeep and carefully examined the rock faces, in some areas with the help of binoculars. Not a scratch except for one or two large-sized Arabic inscriptions painted on the walls of the bed of the gorge.

This spectacular route led toward 'Ein Umm Aḥmed. From a distance this oasis seemed to be all palms, but as we approached over rounded granite rocks we could see the line of the watercourse below us. It was lush with vegetation: rushes, palms, and other trees. The stream ran in a narrow ravine 3 or 4 meters below the granite area where we parked the jeep. In years when there was a lot of rain, the flow of the water was considerable. The rainfall in the southern part of the Sinai had been poor for some years, however, and many of the sources of water were drier than they had been a decade earlier. We had seen this at 'Ein Fortaga several days previously.

As one looked down into the ravine, in some places all that could be seen was the fronds of the palms, while at other points groups of trees stood free and clear. In the watercourse, which runs along the sandy bed of this ravine, were bedouin girls, as always with their flocks. Anat and Tal, our passengers, planned to stay here overnight; we picked them up the next day. The pools in which we hoped to swim had dried up, and it was necessary to go at least a kilometer eastward in the ravine to find a swimming hole. However, there was perpetual flowing water there. One can approach the ravine either from the western end, where we were, or from its eastern end. The western approach was the path that can be followed by vehicle, but on camels or donkeys one can take the other route about 3 or 4 kilometers down the ravine.

Mary and Eyal continued on with us as we drove on from 'Ein Umm Aḥmed, striving to get as close as possible to Wadi Zalaqa before camping.

The information we had about the present location of the border in Wadi Zalaqa was contradictory, and the reports I had received clearly indicated a major collection of inscriptions there. We were determined to do our best to see it. About 5 kilometers south of 'Ein Umm Aḥmed, we encountered a concentration of third- and fourth-millennium BCE sites. The first thing we saw was two stone circles in which were seven standing stones in a row. Here there were numerous third- and fourth-millennium flints (see fig. 24 above).

The wadi that we were traveling was known as Wadi el-'Ein (Wadi of the Spring); older reports, I recall hearing, refer to 'Ein Umm Aḥmed simply as el-'Ein. There are, in Wadi el-'Ein, numerous sandstone rocks and outcroppings of the sort that often bear either inscriptions or rock drawings. We checked the most likely sites, but it was impossible to check every inch of this fascinating area. We observed many stone circles, *nawamis*, and other similar sites in this area south of 'Ein Umm Aḥmed, many from the third millennium BCE. By now it was 6:00 in the evening, and the sun was setting. We bowled along the wadi trying to make as much distance as we could before dark.

At 6:08 we came upon an oval rock standing near the western side of the wadi. Numerous rock drawings decorate the rock, some of them exceptionally finely executed, but we recorded no inscriptions. As the sun set, it silhouetted strikingly the mountains to our west. About half a kilometer from the junction with Wadi Ghalem, we saw a brown rock face to our south with drawings and one Nabatean inscription. Half a kilometer farther, also on the southern side of the wadi, were an Arabic inscription and a few drawings.

The great route that had carried us south from near Eilat now swung around to the southeast. After the junction with Wadi Ghalem, the name of the wadi changed from Wadi el-'Ein to Wadi Zaraniyeh. It was growing dark rapidly, so we proceeded along the wadi quite fast, checking likely sandstone rocks. After a while the sandstone was replaced on all sides by limestone, a type of rock on which there are almost never any inscriptions. The northern wall of the wadi was bounded by low hills; to the south was limestone and occasionally sandstone. Overall this was not the sort of rock formation that usually attracts drawings and inscriptions.

After the light had nearly faded completely away, we camped for the night. It was cooling off. Mary's cooking skills ensured that the brew that was cooking—soup and canned meat with onions and more—smelled appetizing. It was a pleasant spot for the night, up against the southern

6. THE FIFTH EXPEDITION, 14–18 JULY 1980

side of the wadi. As we ate, a large but harmless spider ran across our campsite and disappeared under the jeep. In the morning light, we also saw hyena tracks near the campsite. We refueled the jeep from the reserve jerry cans.

Wadi el-Ḥesi, which we had traversed that day, is a broad, straight, and majestic valley. It is wide at its northern end and gradually narrows as it proceeds south. The complex of wadis of which Wadi Zalaqa is a part is also broad, easily passable, and impressive, although falling short of Wadi el-Ḥesi's majesty. Wadi el-Ḥesi has few inscriptions of any kind and very few rock drawings. This may be partly due to the geological character of its walls, which do not encourage the would-be writer of graffiti or aspiring artist. However, being wary of such explanations, I also thought that it might be due to the clearly marked, ancient track that runs down the center of this wide wadi. A traveler would have to go quite some distance aside in order to find a surface on which to scratch a graffito.

On a second visit (pursuing his jeep that had been stolen; that is another story) Uzi noted one place where the route leaves the wadi, takes a short cut, and rejoins the wadi several kilometers farther on. This detour was a sure sign of an ancient road; a similar detour occurs in Wadi Zalaqa. This once again confirmed the antiquity of that route.

Thursday, 17 July 1980

When I awoke at 5:00 AM, the desert had the light of daybreak on it, and gray clouds covered the heavens. This was a pleasant contrast with the deep, unvarying blue sky of the previous day. In this dawn hour the wind was still cool as it touched our faces. I saw the first rays of the sun shining like a halo over the mountains. Then, at about 5:20, the sun itself appeared. It looked strange: oval-shaped and seemingly cut in two by a bar of clouds. Half an hour later it was rising, strong, promising a hot day. I checked the odometer on the jeep; it stood at 25,625. That meant that since starting we had covered 142 kilometers. Uzi set about fixing the previous day's puncture and checking navigational details. Mary and Eyal got busy with breakfast. We ate, finished up the tire repair, and were on our way by 6:45. I hoped very much that we would be able to get to the area of Wadi Zalaqa, which I knew to contain inscriptions. The problem was the border with Egypt. Where did it pass? On which side of it were the inscriptions?

When we left our camp, we traveled along a wide wadi with walls of mixed sandstone and limestone. There were scattered bushes and rocks on the sandy wadi bed. After a dozen kilometers, at about 7:10, we stopped to verify our position, for the previous evening we had driven the last few kilometers without careful navigation. The wadi was covered with bushes that, crushed under our wheels, gave off a pungent and not unpleasant odor. They were *Artemis judaica*, or wormwood (Hebrew *la'ana*), though of a different type than the European plant so called. The bedouin use this bush as an aroma for their tea. The smell of the bushes was with us still as we entered Wadi Zalaqa at 7:27 AM. From our location there, it was 27 kilometers to the inscriptions. I was excited and a bit tense, particularly fearing that our efforts would be in vain. Thus far we had traveled 15 kilometers from our overnight camp. After progressing roughly 3.5 km farther along Wadi Zalaqa, we observed a major Chalcolithic site on the eastern side at Wadi Abu Tarifiyeh. There were also mines and some additional archaeological sites. We did not go into the mines but proceeded straight along Wadi Zalaqa.

At 8:00, 19 kilometers from the previous night's camp, we came to the not unexpected but nonetheless terribly disappointing location of the border. A fence of barbed wire had been stretched across the wadi from one stone side to the other. Once more, we were frustrated by the implementation of the Israeli-Egyptian agreements in the Sinai.

Not being able to report further on my own visit, which these circumstances cut short, I take the opportunity of relaying the detailed notes that Uzi made on a previous visit to the Wadi Zalaqa area. He had followed a route much like ours and had been able to spend a few hours in the area. To his report, I add some notes on conversations I have had with Shauly, Avner Goren's assistant, who had worked on rock drawings in the same area.

Some short distance from where we stopped was a water source. Uzi noted on his visit that there were flocks, two palm trees, and a built concrete pool. The end of Wadi Zalaqa was wide, with many *hadbes*, great outcroppings of sandstone like those in the area of Wadi Ḥajjaj. Some of these were even the size of the extremely large rock called Umm 'Araq that we had surveyed not far from Naqb Rakna.[10]

There were on the *hadbes* that he had examined predominantly Nabatean inscriptions. There were also Greek inscriptions and a good number of crosses. Uzi copied one Georgian inscription. Some of the

---

10. See above, pages 76–77.

6. THE FIFTH EXPEDITION, 14–18 JULY 1980

inscriptions were quite lightly incised. The inscriptions that he saw were scattered over a large area but also occurred in concentrated groups. He observed three such concentrations. One of the Arabic inscriptions was five lines in length.

Shauly also knew the area and added the following. Uzi had visited, he said, only a small part of the *hadbes* that were inscribed or that bore drawings. In fact, there is an area of several kilometers at the end of Wadi Zalaqa, in the area called Ras Zalaqa (Head of Zalaqa), above the end of the wadi, that is full of inscriptions and drawings. He had even found some drawings done in ochre in a cave not far from there.

I did not see Shauly's photographs of that area. They were only just back from the laboratory and not yet sorted or identified. He himself had not yet seen them when I talked with him in Jerusalem, a few days before I left for the Netherlands. He had been photographing rock drawings, not inscriptions. At exactly the same time at the Israel Museum there was an exhibition about rock drawings, collected by an Italian researcher by the name of Emmanuel Anati. Clearly, he could not present more than a tiny sample of the enormous numbers of rock drawings that exist. I myself must have observed hundreds, if not thousands. Anati did try to set up a typological series of drawings, which is problematic. However, if this typological approach were combined with dating of drawings executed over or under datable inscriptions, I think that the crucial issue of chronology of the rock drawings could be partly resolved.

The results of this chief aspect of our expedition were quite disappointing. We had hoped that the temporary border was farther down the wadi or that we would find at least some representative groups of inscriptions on our side of the border. According to Shauly, who is the only person who has spent any length of time there and who is, at least peripherally interested in inscriptions, there is up to a week's work there. This much is already absolutely clear to me: the route to Mount Sinai via Wadi el-Ḥesi and Wadi Zalaqa was clearly a major one. The Wadi Zalaqa inscriptions are the second chief group of inscriptions in eastern Sinai that our Christian pilgrims left. They seem to be fewer in number than those of Wadi Ḥajjaj, although we should await a thorough study of the whole area before drawing even that conclusion. Among the materials seen, the Christian inscriptions are the minority alongside the Nabatean, and those Christian inscriptions are predominantly Greek. Uzi saw at least one Georgian inscription, and this was probably the one "in your script" that Shauly had told me he saw a year or more before.

The importance of these inscriptions, apart from their intrinsic interest, is that they confirm the route through Wadi el-Ḥesi and the connecting wadis to Ras Zalaqa and from there southward to Mount Sinai through Watiyeh Pass, where we had seen crosses on a previous occasion.

This route has easily available water along Wadi el-Ḥesi. There are two wells between 'Ein Umm Aḥmed and Ras Zalaqa, as well as the water source at the end of Wadi Zalaqa itself. One is a well called Bir Rakaba, the other a well we found unmarked on the map. This route is short, easy to traverse, and available to travelers coming either from Eilat (Aila) or from the direction of Elusa-Nessana.

A second possible north-south route is along the coast (see above). What remains unclear about both routes is the following. On the Wadi el-Ḥesi route, one way to Mount Sinai is to continue by 'Ein Umm Aḥmed (where we found no inscriptions) and Wadi el-'Ein and the Wadi Zalaqa complex. Another possible route is to keep bearing south from Wadi el-Ḥesi, shortly south of Bir es-Sawa, and to proceed through one of a number of possible southern routes to the area of Wadi Ḥajjaj, Wadi Ḥudra, and thence to the high mountains of Saint Catherine's and Mount Sinai.

Of this complex of routes, the only one we could traverse by jeep was Wadi Watir. The others will need to be checked on another occasion, if one offers itself. The routes that can be traversed by vehicles today are not necessarily those taken by ancient pilgrim caravans. Camels and donkeys can travel where jeeps cannot.

A similar uncertainty surrounds the path taken from the coast road inland. Wadi Watir is one possibility that people have considered. In it is the spring of 'Ein Fortaga of which I have written above.[11] The coastal route is witnessed by the inscriptions of Bir Sweir and perhaps by those of Wadi Tweibeh at its northern end. Farther south, the exact route is still something of a mystery. An additional conundrum is that the detailed topography of the area of Wadi Ḥajjaj and the surrounding countryside reveals no reason why that particular spot should have attracted such a major concentration of inscriptions.

Trying to understand the distribution of the inscriptions again raises problems. The use of Wadi el-Ḥesi by pilgrims is confirmed by some inscriptions in Wadi Sidri III at its northern end, as well as by the inscribed

---

11. See above, page 26.

stone we found by the wayside there, and by the single cross discovered at the site of Wadi Sa'ad, about 5 kilometers north of Bir es-Sawa. The crucial evidence, however, is the concentration of inscriptions in Wadi Zalaqa, and here I am unable to tell their numbers or character, except that there is one in Georgian and certainly some in Greek. Their authors must have followed Wadi el-Ḥesi, since there is no other route that could have led into Wadi Zalaqa. However, the length of Wadi el-Ḥesi, like that of the Wadi Zalaqa complex, has almost no inscriptions of any type. This was doubtless a journey of at least several days, so why Wadi Ḥajjaj and not elsewhere? This question still haunts me.

The route given by Theodosius mentions eight days of travel from Aila to Mount Sinai. This was at the beginning of the sixth century CE and certainly before 518 CE. The Piacenza Pilgrim (around 570) also apparently knew this route, for when he describes possible travel routes he says that from Mount Sinai to Aila are eight staging posts.

What is unclear, however, is the actual route he himself followed. He mentions that he was at Elusa in the Negev. From there he traveled 20 miles to the hostel of Saint George. This is usually identified as being at Nessana southwest of Elusa; John Wilkinson in his fascinating book *Jerusalem Pilgrims* observes that it might also be at Obode (Ovdat). From there he traveled in the desert during six days, before encountering a Saracen festival. "Going on through the desert," he continues, "we arrived on the eighth day at the place where Moses brought water out of the rock. A day's journey from there we came to Horeb."[12]

Philip Mayerson, in a paper written some years ago, assumes that the Piacenza Pilgrim traveled from Elusa and Nessana across the Tih Desert and from there to Mount Sinai.[13] This route across the Tih was used, but it was doubtless a difficult one. In the fifteenth century the German Friar Felix Fabri traveled it, and he describes vividly all the suffering it inflicted on his group. It is by no means necessary to assume that the Piacenza Pilgrim went across the Tih. At least one possible alternative (the one Wilkinson seems to accept, to judge from his map 27) is that he traveled through Wadi el-Ḥesi. We have observed that the Eilat-Gaza road crosses the head of the Wadi el-Ḥesi route, which turns southward. A final reso-

---

12. Quoted in John Wilkinson, *Jerusalem Pilgrims before the Crusades* (Jerusalem: Ariel, 1977), 87.

13. Philip Mayerson, "The Desert of Southern Palestine according to Byzantine Sources," *Proceedings of the American Philosophical Society* 107 (1963): 161–62.

lution of this problem can emerge only from future epigraphic surveys and studies.

∗∗

Our next goal was to return to the area of Wadi Ḥajjaj. We had to follow up the Danish man's report of two inscribed *hadbes* near the White Canyon. One necessary step in answering the question of the pilgrim routes was to determine whether from Wadi el-Ḥesi they had gone through ʿEin Fortaga. On previous visits we had found no indications of pilgrim presence at ʿEin Fortaga or on the way between ʿEin Fortaga and the coast, which is the continuation of Wadi Watir, an impressive, winding wadi flanked by high granite cliffs. We now traversed the part of it that runs between Wadi el-Ḥesi and ʿEin Fortaga. We found no inscriptions of any type there either. This confirmed Negev's observations that there are no inscriptions at ʿEin Fortaga. He proffers as a reason the fact that that area was granite and therefore hard to inscribe. Yet in other granite areas there are inscriptions, so Negev's argument is not conclusive.

Wadi Watir's main virtue (other than its great natural beauty), is that it is passable by vehicle. Repeatedly experienced Sinai hands have observed to me that, if they had to travel from Wadi el-Ḥesi to ʿEin Ḥudra and the Ḥajjaj area, they would not take the route by way of Wadi Watir and Wadi Ghazaleh that we followed by jeep. That route is possible, of course, and had to be checked, but a much shorter way is via Wadi Lathy or even the passage through Wadi el-Faris and Wadi el-Bireh. These routes are straight and direct. They pass on the eastern side of Jebel Baraqa and so might explain the inscriptions that I have heard reported from that area, although those are said to be Nabatean. We were unable to check these possibilities, however, so this aspect of the problem remains unsolved. In fact, we had planned an exploration on camel back, but the peace treaty with Egypt and the new border made that impossible.

We drove north from Wadi Zalaqa back to ʿEin Umm Aḥmed. Twenty-four kilometers from the fence that marks the border, we examined a rock on the south side of the wadi and noted drawings there on the sandstone. Just 3 kilometers more were needed for us to see the peak of Jebel Baraqa, and another 4 returned us to the area of Wadi el-ʿEin where we had seen the oval sandstone *hadbe* the previous day. A curiously shaped, free-standing sandstone rock bore a remarkable resemblance to a squatting dog, which led us to nickname it Snoopy. There were rock drawings on Snoopy. A further 4 kilometers along the road brought us to a number of Chalcolithic sites. We traveled about half a kilometer off

6. THE FIFTH EXPEDITION, 14–18 JULY 1980

the main route and observed serried stone heaps along the ridge of a hill, looking for all the world like battlements. Our archaeologists, Uzi and Mary, climbed the hill to examine them. They counted thirteen well-preserved tumuli and two shrines; from the height of the hill they could see many other similar sites, including an ancient dwelling place.

This region was 6 kilometers south of 'Ein Umm Aḥmed. We reached that oasis shortly before 4:00 PM. I climbed down to the watercourse and washed off in the spring of cool water, a most welcome refreshment. The others went off down the ravine to look for Anat and Tal, who had been swimming in the one water hole that was still swimmable (the closer one had dried up).

From there we continued by way of Wadi Watir through 'Ein Fortaga to the coast. We badly needed to refuel the jeep, and the young folk wanted to leave us there. Anat and Tal returned to Eilat, while Mary and Eyal spent the night at Nweiba. They had had their fill of bumping through the desert in the back of a jeep. Uzi and I, however, decided not to sleep at Nweiba, so after taking on fuel and enjoying some ice cream, we immediately set out south along the coast road, on the familiar route to Wadi Sa'al. We intended to survey the general area at the head of the various ascents from 'Ein Ḥudra following up on the clue given to us by the Dane. By the time we turned off the paved road it was completely dark. This was not my first experience of Uzi driving through the desert in the dark. He had an almost uncanny sense of direction, and we drove along the unpaved road as far as a point between the turn off to Wadi Ghazaleh and Wadi Ḥajjaj. We then set our faces to the north and drove a short distance inland, off any sort of track. The territory was sandy, as far as we could make it out in the dark. We found a comfortable spot and camped for the night. It was a quiet evening, just the two of us. We ate and then spent time working on our notes and records and making sure that we had included all the proper information.

As always the desert night was extraordinary—the deep, starry sky, the silence, a wind, and a sense of space around us.

> **SINAI SCENES 12**
> The land's layered love,
> God's wilderness where he is found,
> our wilderness where he is sought.
> Israel, Elijah, and Paul the Monk,
>
> meeting God in desert,
> God stomps from Sinai,
> with his myriad hosts.
> Did Israel's God ever like
> the wet, green, sappy land?
>
> MES

Friday, 18 July 1980

This was the last day of this trip and the end of the field research I intended to do. We arose at 5:00 AM, ate, packed our gear, and generally readied ourselves for the day. I hoped to make the 2:00 plane to Jerusalem from Eilat, for it was Friday, and if I did not catch it there was no certain transport to the capital for another two days, due to the Sabbath and the airline schedules. We set out at 6:20, and our first goal was to head for the sandstone cliffs that were a few hundred meters from our camping spot. It turned out that the previous evening in the dark Uzi had brought us to just about exactly the spot where we wanted to be. We were in Wadi Abu Ghad'ayat (fig. 25). On the rock face I immediately observed a Greek inscription containing a Nabatean name. It was unlikely to be Christian. I followed the rocks to the east while Uzi fixed a sudden puncture. Checking all these great sandstone cliffs, I observed Nabatean and Arabic inscriptions along the rock face that I followed until it reached the unpaved road. Wadi Abu Ghad'ayat is near the exit from Wadi Ghazaleh, as well as near the exit from the White Canyon and 'Ein Ḥudra, and is as logical a place for travelers to camp as Wadi Ḥajjaj.

We surveyed other rocks in this area and found evidence of pilgrim traffic in the form of crosses scattered throughout. There were drawings, as well as Nabatean and Arabic inscriptions on a number of other *hadbes* in this area.

Then we advanced toward the top of the old ascent from 'Ein Ḥudra to Wadi Ḥajjaj. At the top of the pass we saw "footsteps" and drawings on

6. THE FIFTH EXPEDITION, 14–18 JULY 1980

Fig. 25. Uzi and the jeep at Jebel Abu Ghad'ayat

a flat rock. The inscriptions were concentrated in particular on the *hadbes* south-southeast of the head of the pass. This raised at least two possible scenarios. Perhaps the pilgrims ascended from 'Ein Ḥudra and Wadi Ḥudra via the pass. Alternatively, they may have come by way of Wadi Ghazaleh and remained by these rocks while their guides went down to 'Ein Ḥudra to bring water.

We completed our work in this area, having surveyed the *hadbes* at the head of Wadi Abu Ghad'ayat in the general direction of south to north (fig. 26). This took us until 8:30 AM; according to the odometer we had covered 10 kilometers.

We then decided to return to Wadi Ḥajjaj. I wished to reexamine Rock VIII there, which we had identified on our last visit; I also had long wished to complete the survey of the northern part of this wadi, between the modern pass down to 'Ein Ḥudra and Rock III. Here we had already discovered a number of inscribed rocks that Negev had not noted.

The northernmost rock in the wadi is a large *hadbe*. On it we found some rock drawings, some old Arabic inscriptions, and one inscription in a script we could not identify. We gave this rock the number XI. Soon after we found inscriptions on another, unlisted site, which we called Rock XII. It was just south and slightly east of Rock XI and bore drawings and a single

Fig. 26. Wadi Abu Ghad'ayat

Nabatean inscription. We then searched for some time until we rediscovered Rock VIII. The inscriptions are on its eastern face and are very badly weathered. Now, at the end of my Sinai travels, I rediscovered the very first inscription I had ever found there. The four Armenian letters were clear enough. The rock also had Greek and Nabatean and some drawings. Abraham Negev particularly wanted photographs of the Nabatean inscriptions of this rock, and I would gladly have given them to him, but they were so badly weathered that they were indecipherable. In any case, this group of three rocks should be added to the corpus that Negev published.

Having completed the survey of this area, we proceeded to the east. We checked Rock X again and the areas around it. Once more we failed to find Negev's Rock IX. However, a new discovery still awaited us, to end the day's work with a bang. This was Rock XIII, which is in the western part of Wadi Ḥajjaj not far from Rock X. It is quite remarkable in shape, being a long, low rock on which sit large cubes of stone, just like a couple of wooden blocks. As we approached it, we saw inscriptions and rock drawings. These were in Greek and Nabatean, and some of them were Christian (fig. 27).

Drawing nearer, I found an absolutely beautifully carved Georgian inscription and below it a single Georgian letter. This handsome rock and its inscriptions make a fine addition to the corpus from this area. We photographed and measured all that had to be photographed and measured, then briefly checked some *hadbes* north and west of Rock X, which had Arabic inscriptions and drawings. At 11:24 we exited from the unpaved road onto the main road north.

Appropriately, I ended the last field trip of this project where I had started, partly out of curiosity, more than a year before: at Wadi Ḥajjaj. The problems of the pilgrim routes were still partly unsolved, but we had managed not only to throw some light on the routes followed by Armenian pilgrims to the Sinai but also to clarify a good deal about the pilgrim routes in eastern Sinai in general. Certain desiderata remained beyond our reach, as must always be the case, but the main lines of research seemed to be clear, and now the tasks of decipherment and publication lay ahead.

The trip back to Eilat went smoothly, as did the flight back to Jerusalem. After my return I set about gathering additional information about the inscriptions in eastern Sinai. That story is not ended nor those riches exhausted. However, barring the unexpected—always a possibility—the greater part of the material about the Armenians has been collected and photographed. Zev had the proofs of his photos when I got back. They

Fig. 27. Wadi Ḥajjaj, Rock XIII with Nabatean and rock drawings

were excellent; some were better than those we already had, others not quite as good. Rock III is, indeed, exceedingly difficult to photograph.

The day before I left Jerusalem for a year in the Netherlands, I went over to the Church of the Holy Sepulchre. There on the pillars outside the entrance were dozens of Armenian graffiti. They were all in a much later script and style than the Sinai ones, and we know that those pillars were erected in the twelfth century under the Crusader kings of Jerusalem. This is a valuable and easily understood reference point for dating Armenian graffiti of the Holy Land or elsewhere.

Before I departed, I had the graphic work for the publication prepared and went through considerable contortions to get an aerial photograph of the Wadi Ḥajjaj area (fig. 2). Further study of the inscriptions also had to be completed, and their implications for Armenian history and writing needed to be drawn. I tried to carry out these imperatives in the following years and published the Sinai finds with detailed commentary and discussion. The question of the east Sinai travel routes, in particular the gathering of information from the area of Ras Zalaka, remains open. I shall remember the experience, the sights, and the beauty of the Sinai Peninsula all my life.

7
NEGEV DIARY
19–21 APRIL 1990

During the decade from 1980 to 1990 my energies were devoted to gathering as much photographic evidence of the Sinai inscriptions as I could. The Egyptians gave no access to the inner desert of the Sinai. I mourned the fact that Israeli archaeologists had not done surveys of graffiti, systematically photographing sites such as Wadi Mukattab. This could have been done easily during the decade that the Sinai was in Israeli hands.

As I worked out the implications of our finds, I realized that the issues concerned not just Armenian pilgrims but all Christian pilgrimage. In addition, the mysteries of the Nabateans became more acute. I had also assembled a great deal of information about desert travel.

The first need was to gather information from experienced Sinai hands in the period directly after the withdrawal, when their memories were still fresh. I also put out the word that we were seeking pictures of any inscriptions people had photographed in the Sinai. Avner Goren, for one, made many pictures available.

I developed the Rock Inscriptions and Graffiti Project to organize and archive all the available images of Sinai inscriptions. In the printed catalogue of the project, published in 1992–1994, I gave details of about nine thousand epigraphs of the Sinai material we had gathered.[1] Afterward we collected photographs and graffiti from various holy places and pilgrimage sites in the Holy Land. Could we find the same people visiting, for example, in Jerusalem and at Jebel Musa? The rest of the decade was

---

1. Michael E. Stone, *Rock Inscriptions and Graffiti Project: Catalogue of Inscriptions*, 3 vols., Resources for Biblical Studies 28–29, 31 (Atlanta: Scholars Press, 1992–1994).

devoted to photographic expeditions to these places and processing the data assembled.

A team of young assistants entered this information into a computer at the level of sophistication then available. By the mid-1980s, the money was coming to an end, and we decided to mount an expedition to the southern Negev Desert of Israel, where Uzi had seen interesting inscriptions.

On this trip, as I have done in the past, I kept a personal journal, in addition to the scientific documentation. With me were three others: Uzi, his assistant Rina, and my fourteen-year-old son Dan. This was Dan's first experience of desert work, and he was an enormous help.

Thursday, 19 April 1990

We departed Jerusalem at 6:00 AM in a heavily loaded jeep and drove south. After three hours, we came to the 'Ein Ovdat turn off from the road to Eilat. Ovdat was a Nabatean city, later Christian, and part of the extensive Nabatean settlement of the northern Negev. 'Ein Ovdat (Spring of Ovdat) is an oasis in a deep cleft with plentiful water. The spring there was running strong, yet notices forbade swimming. The water is saline, and the plants are salt-loving. The cleft was green with vegetation, but the hills were stony and barren. We set out to walk from 'Ein Ovdat to the city of Ovdat itself in search of rocks with North Arabic inscriptions and drawings that Uzi had seen on an earlier visit to this site.

We found inscriptions of types different from those we had seen in the course of our Sinai expeditions. In the Sinai we had discovered graffiti left by Christian pilgrims en route to the holy sites of Mount Sinai, traveling either from Jerusalem in the north or from Egypt in the south. We had deciphered their names in many tongues, in Greek and Latin, in Armenian and Georgian, in Syriac and Ethiopic, in English and Bulgarian. Indeed, pilgrims still go there. We did not expect many pilgrim inscriptions on this Negev trip, for the site that beckoned us was not on a pilgrim route.

We expected to see inscriptions written by the nomadic inhabitants of these wildernesses. These were Old North Arabic (a linguistic forebear of classical and modern Arabic), Nabatean, and Arabic. In addition, many of these nomadic people left drawings on the rocks, often crude but occasionally of remarkable sensitivity. Conquerors and exploiters were always ephemeral in this wilderness world, yet they left other inscriptions. Some of the Arabic epigraphs fell into this category, some of the Greek and Latin ones, as well as the Egyptian hieroglyphs that were familiar from the Sinai. What would the Negev yield?

We were in the rocky area between 'Ein Ovdat and Ovdat searching for limestone laced with flint, which develops a dark patina or surface coloring. The type of rock affects the type of inscriptions. The softest rock is sandstone, which is plentiful in the Sinai. Over the centuries sandstone develops a dark patina that shows incisions clearly. In the Ovdat area, however, Uzi had seen inscriptions not on sandstone but on patinaed limestone. We set out on foot proceeding parallel to the bed of Naḥal Ovdat, the deep canyon in which the water flowed. This part of it, higher than the spring, was dry. We discovered a series of brown patinaed rocks along the course of the wadi upon which we saw rock drawings of ibex, camels, and human figures, as well as *wasem*s (bedouin tribal markings) and inscriptions. One inscription was in an unknown script, perhaps badly written Arabic, another clearly in Old North Arabic, over which were other fainter inscriptions. By now it was 11:20 in the morning.

The bedouin markings are widespread in the Negev and Sinai. Palmer relates the following incident that illustrates their function. His guide wished to leave a notice for the following camel drivers indicating where they were going. To do so, he left his tribal mark, a footstep, and their tribal mark.[2] This is perhaps the meaning of the "footsteps" we saw in the Sinai.

Our visit was in April, and there were pools of stagnant water left from the winter along the bed of the wadi. At one moment we saw seven birds of prey in the sky at once, including an eagle, two buzzards, and vultures. It was spring, so we also observed migrating storks and many flowering plants. The desert was covered with flowers of different colors—white and purple and yellow—as well various sorts of plants.

Uzi and his assistant Rina returned from the farthest point at which we found inscriptions to bring the jeep. Dan and I continued to survey on foot along the bed of Naḥal Ovdat until we reached Ovdat. On the way we saw rather interesting white chalk rock formations, like miniature white cliffs of Dover.

Leaving this area, we drove to Mitzpeh Ramon. This small town is on the edge of the great Ramon Crater, one of the major geological (and scenic) features of the Negev Desert. In winter one hears about it snowing

---

2. Edward H. Palmer, *The Desert of the Exodus: Journeys on Foot in the Wilderness of the Forty Years' Wanderings* (Cambridge: Deighton & Bell, 1871), 253.

there. It had a certain "frontier" quality, as do many of the smaller settlements in the south. We took on food and provisions and by 12:40 were en route from Mitzpeh Ramon to the western road that runs down through the Negev near the Egyptian border. By the road we observed a bush of the same variety as is found at Saint Catherine's Monastery, where it is believed to be a scion of the biblical burning bush. In general it looked a bit like a bramble, and it is called *Bladder senna* or *Colutea istria* (Hebrew *karkas tsahov*).

The countryside was hilly. There are trees known as Atlantic pistachios that are green and are properly native to wetter areas than the Negev. They grow there, however, remnants of the vegetation from a period during which the Negev was much wetter. Most of the area, however, comprises brown hills dotted with low bushes.

The nomadic Nabateans lived in the Negev, southern Jordan, the Arabian Peninsula, and the Sinai, where we had encountered many traces of them. In the last centuries BCE they became active traders and built great cities in the desert, one of which was Ovdat. Another, the most famous, was Petra in southern Jordan. Their routes of travel interested us because they left many graffiti by the side of their routes, and certain of those routes led nowhere obvious.

We were heading for Mount Karkom. Recently Italian archaeologist Emanuel Anati proposed that this is the biblical Mount Sinai. He published books to propagate his theory, which has not met with much acceptance.[3] But clearly the site is significant, and Anati's photographs of drawings, combined with information Uzi had about inscriptions, made it the chief goal of our expedition.

About a mile from the base of Mount Karkom, we saw a rock with inscriptions on it. We do not take rubbings or latex impressions because the surface of the rock is usually very friable and the patina easily damaged. Anati, in his surveys, found numerous rock epigraphs of Neolithic vintage. Our job was to check for any Armenian or other Christian pilgrim graffiti.

We camped for the night on a flat, rocky area at the base of Mount Karkom, which is a ridge 4.5 kilometers long and 850 meters high. The ground is not the clean sand of the eastern Sinai but friable earth. We

---

3. See, e.g., Emanuel Anati, *Har Karkom, The Mountain of God* (New York: Rizzoli, 1986).

cleared stones and slept there. I woke at 3:00 AM and got my view of the desert sky. I observed that there were no mosquitos or insects; there never are in this desert, except in parts of the southern Sinai near the coast. During the night there was some rain, but by morning the skies were clear and blue. It looked as though it would be sunny.

Friday, 20 April 1990

Near where we slept for the night were two small rocks on which there were rock drawings and a *wasem*. I photographed them first thing in the morning. Uzi and I discussed some of the strange symbolic signs in the rock drawings. He pointed out the relationship between these and some of the large rock pictures drawn, using stones to outline them. Some such pictures found in the Negev were as large as 2 kilometers across. He suggests that the great rock pictures reflect the symbolic rock drawings and that some of them may have phallic or other fertility significance.

By 7:30 we had eaten breakfast, packed up, and were ready to go. Ahead there were several mountains, each of which forms a part of the extended range of Mount Karkom. We were at the base of the main ascent, and our plan was to climb the middle of the three peaks we saw before us.

The ascent to Mount Karkom was steep and quite difficult but not very long. It took about half an hour. The ridge of this mountain bore the character of a hilly plateau of earth covered with stones. Flint implements were lying around. Once we reached the plateau, we had a walk of an hour or an hour and a half to reach an area that was marked by a large series of outcroppings of darkly patinaed limestone. This rocky area stretched the length of a valley on the mountaintop plateau, which ran from north to south. It was covered with groups of rocks on which we found large numbers of rock drawings, various signs, and inscriptions in North Arabic writing. Usually these North Arabic inscriptions are graffiti of merely one or two words, giving a personal name.

We did not photograph everything, only the most interesting or unusual rock drawings and all of the inscriptions that we could find. Our survey was far from exhaustive. Nonetheless, we must have taken about forty or fifty frames of film in that area. The dominant subjects were ibex and groups of ibex together with a dog, themes that were repeated frequently. We observed two pictures of a man and a woman in an orans (praying) position. We also noticed an unusual serpentine sort of sign splitting into two parts at one end, which was repeated on a number of rocks. There were various other apparently symbolic signs whose meaning we could not guess. Another thing that was unusual about the corpus of materials on Mount Karkom was the absence of Nabatean inscriptions. There were no Christian inscriptions either and no hint of any other language. We found one quite old Arabic inscription, but I saw no recent Arabic.

We examined only one area of this mountain ridge, which is several kilometers long and well worth further work in the field. We did not exhaust even that one area examined, and there are surely other such concentrations elsewhere along that mountain ridge. Why the inscriptions were written there and what their significance is for the history of humans in the Negev wilderness remain mysterious. The mountain has been characterized as a cult place, a term that often obscures more than it clarifies.

After the descent from Mount Karkom in mid-afternoon, we drove to the Uvda Valley, an important site not too far from Eilat. Uzi had done extensive work on desert agriculture and the religion of Chalcolithic peoples, which is evidenced by their archaeological remains in that area. We were keen to see two sites in the Uvda Valley. The first was a white chalk rock, quite large and standing on its own. On it was an odd inscription, the first two letters of which seemed to resemble Armenian but were not, while the other letters looked like European Latin writing. However, it did not seem to make any sense. On the same face of the rock were some rock drawings and other signs, perhaps Greek letters. I photographed these, and we then proceeded to another site within the same wadi. At the second site we also found strange scratchings and apparently parts of a Greek inscription on a rock.

We left the Uvda Valley and proceeded south toward Eilat, turning off to the left of the road hoping to view a site with some standing stones. The jeep got stuck in two deep ruts, and it took a good deal of digging and effort to get it out. Eventually we reached the standing stones after nightfall. We slept in Eilat, and the next morning Uzi and I worked on the descriptions of the sites and their coordinates and on drafting a report of the archaeological materials we had found.

Saturday, 21 April 1990

In mid-morning we set out for the area of Timna to see some inscriptions there. This is a famous spot north of Eilat, west of the main road, that attracts many tourists. In antiquity, the ancient Egyptians had exploited its copper deposit, and mining operations were resumed in recent times.

In the Timna region we visited several sites. The first was a large sloping rock that had probably fallen down or over. On the underface of this rock we saw a Greek inscription including Eutyche Despota (Mistress Good Fortune) in a frame. We had to lie on our backs and crawl in to see these inscriptions. We also found extensive drawings and other markings on this partially hidden surface. Previous scholars, it seems, had not noted most of these inscriptions. The second site we visited, which is well known, had extensive Egyptian rock drawings, including some of chariots. At a third site close by, a series of rock drawings was visible high up. The ground level has receded greatly, and we could see signs on the rock massif of the old ground level. The signs were way above our heads as we stood at the rock's base.

At Timna we next made for another site, the Roman Cave. In this cave we photographed a number of Greek inscriptions that Uzi knew, at least one of which included a Graecized form of a Nabatean name. Such Nabatean Greek inscriptions are not unusual. Close by the Greek inscriptions of Roman and Nabatean origin, I happened to chance upon a tiny inscription reading Michael in Greek. I also observed a cross in this cave, indicating the presence of Christians there, perhaps as miners.

The fifth site we visited in the Timna Valley was the large Egyptian relief and inscription high in the rock above the Temple of the Goddess Hathor. This "brought home" the extent of the ancient Egyptian economic activities in the area. All of this took us from about 10:30 in the morning until after 2:00 PM, at which time we returned to Eilat, had lunch, and then departed on the 5:00 plane for Jerusalem.

The expedition was rather successful, and we photographed nearly two hundred new inscriptions and rock drawings. We incorporated these into the collection of the Rock Inscriptions Project in Jerusalem. The work in the Negev is far from finished, and extensive survey and photographic work still remains. The material we assembled must be studied and integrated with other bodies of knowledge, both archaeological and written. The inscriptions from the Sinai and from many of the holy places have already been catalogued, and the first volumes of the printed catalogue are in the final stages of preparation as I now write in the spring of 1991.[4] The really good news, however, is that I have the most persuasive reasons to go back to the desert.

---

4. It appeared in three volumes in 1992–1994.

8
Retrospective, 2016

This story is unfinished. As I write these words, at a remove of thirty-seven years from the earliest of the events related, I still am unclear about the routes the pilgrims took, about the reasons for the extraordinary concentration of epigraphs at Wadi Ḥajjaj, and about what may or may not be at Ras Zalaqa. With the help of two experts, I published the Armenian, Georgian, and Latin inscriptions in a book with many further details of routes and other observations.

I managed to show that certain of the Wadi Ḥajjaj inscriptions were the oldest surviving Armenian writing in the world. The publication of that raised a sensation among historians of Armenia and the Holy Land. In the 1980s I assembled all the photographs I could of my own, from Uzi, from Avner Goren, and from others and built a database of them. A catalogue of the database was published, and in 2013 this data resource was mounted on the internet, housed by the Hebrew University of Jerusalem. Thus, at least, this aspect of the Sinai as it was between 1979 and 1980 and some information about pilgrims to the holy places of Christianity will be available to scholars. The URL of that site, designed by Ephraim Damboritz, is: http://rockinscriptions.huji.ac.il.

Uzi has since married Rina, still lives in Eilat, and still works in desert archaeology in the Negev. He has written important studies on the prehistoric inhabitants of the desert. We are in touch regularly. Bill Adler is now Professor of Religion at North Carolina State University. His research concentrates on Byzantine Greek chronographers, and I see him whenever I am in that area. Tom Samuelian finished his doctorate at the University of Pennsylvania and went on to Harvard Law School after teaching Armenian studies at Columbia University in New York for a time. He subsequently settled in Armenia, where he not only has a flourishing law practice but is also Dean of Humanities and Social Sciences at the American University of Armenia. A common friend who visited Saint Catherine's not long ago met Fathi, a patriarchal figure now, married with children.

In the 1970s I was Adjunct Professor of Armenian Studies at the University of Pennsylvania while Vartan Gregorian was Provost and highly respected by faculty and students. On more than one occasion his personal standing in the University community defused crises and student strikes. A couple of years after the events described in this record, he went on to serve as President of the New York Public Library, then as President of Brown University in Rhode Island; now he is President of the Carnegie Corporation.

I myself have retired from the Hebrew University, where I taught for many years as Professor of Armenian Studies and Religion. My vivid interest in Armenian matters, including inscriptions, continues. Years after the events narrated here, something happened that took my mind back to the Sinai. In the 1980s, I was studying some plastered stones discovered under a mosaic floor in Nazareth in the course of building the new Basilica of the Annunciation there. These stones can be dated before the year 447 CE, for an earthquake damaged the floor in that year. Not only did they contain Armenian graffiti, but two of the individuals from the Nazareth stones, I realized with a shock, had also written their names in Wadi Ḥajjaj. Now I could say definitely what I had not dared write before, that the oldest of the Armenian graffiti from the Sinai were written only decades after the invention of the Armenian alphabet in 401. They are the oldest known Armenian writing anywhere.

Bibliography

The following bibliography is heterogeneous. It contains a number of entries on the inscriptions of the south of Israel and the Sinai. In addition, I have added some works on pilgrimage to the Holy Land, as well as on ancient desert cultures. Certain ancient pilgrim reports (*itineraria*) are mentioned, such as that of Egeria, and the reports of the most famous modern scientific travelers, such as Burckhardt, who was the first Westerner to see Petra, and W. M. Flinders Petrie, who uncovered most of the ancient Egyptian antiquities of the Sinai.

Anati, Emanuel. *Har Karkom, the Mountain of God.* New York: Rizzoli, 1986.
Avner, Uzi. "Ancient Cult Sites in the Negev and the Sinai Deserts." *Tel Aviv* 11 (1984): 115–31.
Burckhardt, John Lewis. *Travels in Syria and the Holy Land.* London: Murray, 1822.
Bernstein, Burton. *Sinai: The Great and Terrible Wilderness.* New York: Viking, 1979.
Cooney John D. "Major MacDonald, A Victorian Romantic." *Journal of Egyptian Archeology* 58 (1972): 280–85.
Deveresse, Robert. "Le christianisme dans la péninsule sinaïtique, des origines à l'arrivée des musulmans." *Revue biblique* 49 (1940): 205–23.
Euting, Julius. *Sinaïtische Inschriften.* Berlin: Reimer, 1891.
Fabri, Felix. *Felix Fabri (Circa 1480–1483 A.D.).* Translated by Aubrey Stewart. 2 vols. in 4 London: Palestine Pilgrims' Text Society, 1893–1896.
Folberg, Neil. *In a Desert Land: Photographs of Israel, Egypt, and Jordan.* New York: Abbeville, 1998.
Forsyth, George H., and Kurt Weitzmann. *The Monastery of Saint Catherine at Mount Sinai: The Church and Fortress of Justinian.* Ann Arbor: University of Michigan Press, 1973.
Galey, John. *Sinai and the Monastery of St. Catherine.* Givatayim, Israel: Massada, 1980.

Hazelton, Lesley. *Where Mountains Roar: A Personal Report from the Sinai and the Negev Desert*. New York: Holt, Rinehart & Winston, 1980.

Hirschfeld, Yizhar. *The Judean Desert Monasteries in the Byzantine Period: Their Development and Internal Organization in the Light of Archaeological Research*. Jerusalem: Hebrew University, 1988.

Kraemer, Casper J., Jr. *Excavations at Nessana III: Non-literary Papyri*. Princeton: Princeton University Press, 1958.

Lachish, Ilan, and Ze'ev Meshel. *South Sinai Researches 1967–1982* [Hebrew]. Tel-Aviv: South Sinai Administration and Nature Protection Society, 1982.

Mayerson, Philip. "The Pilgrim Routes to Mount Sinai and the Armenians." *Israel Exploration Journal* 32 (1982): 44–57.

Mayerson, Philip. "The Desert of Southern Palestine according to Byzantine Sources." *Proceedings of the American Philosophical Society* 107 (1963): 160–72.

Meshel, Ze'ev, and Israel Finkelstein. *Antiquities of the Sinai* [Hebrew]. Tel Aviv: HaKibbutz HeMeuhad, 1980.

Nau, François. "Le texte grec des récits du moine Anastase sur les saints pères du Sinaï." *Oriens Christianus* 2 (1902): 58–89.

Negev, Abraham. *The Inscriptions of Wadi Haggag, Sinai*. Qedem 6. Jerusalem: Institute of Archaeology, 1977.

Nickel, Douglas R. *Francis Frith in Egypt and Palestine: A Victorian Photographer Abroad*. Princeton: Princeton University Press, 2004.

Palmer, Edward H. *The Desert of the Exodus: Journeys on Foot in the Wilderness of the Forty Years' Wanderings*. Cambridge: Deighton & Bell, 1871.

Petrie, W. M. Flinders. *Researches in Sinai*. New York: Dutton, 1906.

Prescott, H. F. M. *Once to Sinai: The Further Pilgrimage of Friar Felix Fabri*. New York: Macmillan, 1958.

Puech, Émile. "Une inscription éthiopienne ancienne au Sinaï (Wadi Hajjaj)." *Revue biblique* 87 (1980): 597–600.

Reiner, Elchanan. "Pilgrims and Pilgrimage to Eretz Israel" [Hebrew]. PhD diss. Hebrew University, 1988.

Rothenberg, Benno. "An Archaeological Survey of South Sinai: First Season 1967/1968, Preliminary Report." *Palestine Exploration Quarterly* 102 (1970): 4–29.

———. *God's Wilderness: Discoveries in Sinai*. London: Thames & Hudson, 1961.

———. *Timna, Valley of the Biblical Copper Mines*. London: Thames & Hudson, 1972.

Smith Lewis, Agnes. *In the Shadow of Sinai: A Story of Travel and Research from 1895 to 1897*. Cambridge: Cambridge University Press, 2012.

Stanley, Arthur Penrhyn. *Sinai and Palestine in Connection with Their History*. London: Murray, 1856.

Stone, Michael E. *Armenian Inscriptions from Sinai: Intermediate Report with Notes on Georgian and Nabatean Inscriptions*. Sydney: Maitland, 1979.

———, ed. *The Armenian Inscriptions from the Sinai*. With appendixes on the Georgian and Latin Inscriptions by Michel van Esbroeck and William Adler. Harvard Armenian Texts and Studies 6. Cambridge: Harvard University Press, 1982.

———. "Armenian Inscriptions of the Fifth Century From Nazareth." *Revue des Études Arméniennes* 22 (1990): 315–22.

———. "The Greek Background of Some Sinai Armenian Pilgrims and Some Other Observations." Pages 194–202 in *Medieval Armenian Culture*. Edited by Michael E. Stone and Thomas J. Samuelian. University of Pennsylvania Armenian Texts and Studies 6. Chico, CA: Scholars Press, 1984.

———. "Sinai Armenian Inscriptions." *Biblical Archaeologist* 45 (1981): 27–31.

———. *Rock Inscriptions and Graffiti Project: Catalogue of Inscriptions*. 3 vols. Resources for Biblical Studies 28–29, 31. Atlanta: Scholars Press, 1992–1994.

Thesiger, Wilfred. *Arabian Sands*. New York: Dutton, 1959.

Wilkinson, John. *Jerusalem Pilgrims before the Crusades*. Jerusalem: Ariel, 1977.

INDEX

This index contains the names of ancient and modern persons mentioned in the book as well as all place names and chief subjects discussed.

1 Kings, book of 17:6, 104
'Abbas Pasha, 100, 101, 111
    Abbas Pasha path, 101, 103
Adler, William (Bill), 18, 44, 91, 96, 105, 106, 109–12, 121
Africa, 39
airport, Atarot, 97
Akaba, 39
Albright Institute of Archaeology, 5
Alexander II, Czar, 9, 115
almonds, Sinai, 112
Amalek, 37
Anastasius of Sinai, 7
Anati, Emmanuel, 143, 156
Anatolia, 1
Andrews University, 5
animals,
    acomys russatus, 109
    camels, 132
    fox, 77
    gazelles, 134
    hyena, 141
    ostriches, 26
    panthers, extinct, 84
Arabian peninsula, 156
Aramaic language, 17, 18
Archaeological Staff Officer, 19, 37
ark of the covenant, 80
Armenia, 1
Armenian Church, 116
Armenian Patriarchate of Jerusalem, 105
Armenians, in the Holy Land, 7
Asia Minor, 6
Australia,
    acacias in, 81
    central, 14
Avner, Uzi, *passim*
Avner, Yael, 124, 133
Ayers Rock, 14
Bailey, Clinton, 87
bedouin, 7
    agriculture, 49, 64, 69, 86, 128, 129
    at 'Ein Aḥdar, 69, 70
    at Bir el-Ḥesi, 135
    attitudes to, 87, 88
    auto repair, 82, 86
    center, 37, 46
    children, 111
    conditions of, 96, 100
    encampment, 81
    expectations of, 85
    hospitality of, 39, 40, 42
    in Arabian peninsula, 88
    kiosk run by, 14, 16
    sacrifices, 106
    Saint Catherine's area, 34, 35
    Saint Catherine's area, relationship with monks, 30, 31, 100, 110
    supplies given to, 110
    tribes, Jebaliyeh, 30

bedouin (*cont.*)
  tribes, Muzeineh, 129
  tribes, Tarabin, 129
  watchmen, 19, 23, 41, 85, 124
  way of life, changes in, 84, 85
  women shepherds, 110, 112, 114, 139
Ben Gurion airport, 11, 69
Bernstein, Burton, 30, 87
Berrien Springs, Michigan, 5
Bir Dakur, 83
Bir el-Ḥesi, 135
Bir es-Sawa, 144
  description of, 138
Bir Iqna, 72
Bir Rakaba, 144
Bir Sa'al, 31, 58, 61
Bir Sheikh Suleyman, 83, 84
  description of, 84
Bir Sweir, 131, 144
  inscriptions, 133
birds,
  black kite (*Milvus migrans*), 72
  buzzard, 155
  eagle, 155
  Egyptian vulture, 17, 70, 72
  ostrich, extinct, 84
  ravens, 72, 104
  storks, 155
  tracks of in sand, 77
  vultures, 155
Black Sea, 1
Blake, Robert, 59
Bogharian, Archbishop Norayr, 105, 118
British Museum, 116
Buller, Bob, 2
Burckhardt, J. L., 16, 31, 37, 39, 49, 83, 90, 91, 127
Burning Bush, Chapel of the, 33
Byzantium, 96
Cairo, 33
Canyon of Inscriptions, 134
Caspian Sea, 1
Caucasus, 1
cocylinth, 130
Codex Sinaiticus, 116

Constantine, Emperor, 1
Constantius, Emperor, 1
Cooney, John D., 42
Coral Island (Jezirat Farun), 12, 124
Cross, Frank M., Jr., 123
crosses, 48, 51, 62, 63, 78, 79, 82, 79, 91, 126, 132, 138, 145, 148, 159
Crusaders, 12
  insignia, 91, 115
Cyrus, 17
Darb el Ḥajj, 134
Darb el-Shawi, 134
Darb Gaza, 134
Darius, 17
daybreak, 141
decipherment, difficulties of, 60, 107
Deir el-Arba'in, monastery, 48, 62, 89, 90, 93, 102, 111–13
desert, vulnerability of, 14
Dionysius, Father, 115
DiTommaso, L., 2
Doughty, Charles M., 36, 87
driving, difficulties of, 75, 147
drought, 129, 130, 139
dust, 17, 97
Edom, mountains of, 124
Egeria, pilgrim, 6, 33, 62
Egypt, 6, 22, 34, 39
Egypt-Israel peace agreement, 95
  implications of, 122, 123
  problems caused by, 95, 142
  temporary borders, 69, 95, 97, 98, 140–42
Egyptian antiquities, 42
Egyptian rule in Sinai, 55, 67
  limits for Israeli research, 67, 69
Egyptians, 16, 159
Eilat (Aila), 9, 11–14, 26, 27, 30, 53, 65, 69, 92, 122, 124, 131, 144, 148, 151
  airport, 27, 118
  Gulf of, 11, 12
'Ein Aḥdar, 69, 70
'Ein Fortaga, oasis, 26, 32, 122, 126, 129, 130, 139, 146, 147
'Ein Ḥudra, 127, 146, 147–49

'Ein Ḥudra (cont.)
    bedouin at, 129–30
    description of, 16, 83, 128, 129
    survey of, 121
'Ein Ovdat, 154, 155
'Ein Umm Aḥmed, 138, 144, 146, 147
    description of, 139
Elijah
    Chapel of, 93, 108
    Vale of, 48, 104, 105, 108, 109, 112
Elusa (Halutza), 122, 145
Esbroeck, Michel van, 18, 94, 121
Ethiopic language, 58
Eutaktos, pilgrim, 1, 6
Euting, Julius, 29, 36, 48, 50, 52
Exodus, book of, 80
    15:23–25, 138
    25:10, 81
    25:13, 81
Fathi,
    driver, 30, 31, 43, 44, 46, 51, 55, 57, 61, 62, 65, 96
    home visit to, 87
Feiran (Pharan),
    oasis of, 18, 51, 61
    bedouin center in, 46
Felix Fabri, 6, 62, 64, 73, 83, 84, 130, 132, 145
Field School, Saint Catherine's, 34, 48, 52, 53, 95, 110, 111, 114
Finkelstein, Israel, 112
fish, dried, 127
Fjord, 12, 124
flights, difficulties of, 96
flint, 76, 135, 137, 140, 157
floods, 63
Folberg, Neil, 16, 34, 58
"footprints," 89, 138, 148
footsteps, function of, 155
Forsythe, George, 114
Frieden, Roie, 2
Frith, Francis, 59
Frumin, Mitia, 2
funding, 9, 27, 67, 118, 119, 123
Galey, John, 30

Galicia (Spain), 6
Gaza, 68
geology, 79, 80, 139. *See also* mines
    mineral deposits, 80
Georgian, Georgians, 8
Goren, Avner, 8, 12, 18, 27, 30, 31, 35, 36, 38, 51, 61, 84, 95, 96, 103, 112, 114, 119, 122, 123
graffiti, Armenian, 152
granite, 26, 54, 79, 129, 138, 146
Greek Orthodox Patriarchate of Jerusalem, 33
Greek,
    Greeks, 8
    language, 8
Gregorian, Vardan, 67
hadbe (sandstone boulder), 22, 55, 126, 127, 142, 143, 148, 149, 151
Hajar el-La'awa, rock, 71, 72
Harvard Semitic Museum, 59, 123
Hathor, goddess, temple of, 159
Hazelton, Lesley, 87
Hazeroth, 16, 17
heat, 83, 124, 125, 129, 135
Hebrew University, 5
    Institute of Jewish Studies, 123
Hebrew, language, 17, 18
Hejjaz, 17
hermitage, 102
Ḥmed, driver, 17, 69, 72, 75, 77, 80, 85, 86
holy men and women, 64
holy places, 48, 64
Holy Sepulchre, Church of the, 152
Hoskins, Franklin E., 83, 84
inscription H Arm 18, 19, 20, 21, 39–42, 56, 66, 71, 73
inscription L Arm 3, 50
inscription M Georg 1, 2, 42, 45
inscription M Lat 1, 2, 44
inscription S Arm 1, 105
inscriptions, 143, 149
    Arabic, 17, 37, 40, 42, 47, 48, 55, 56, 59, 63, 134 135, 138, 140, 148, 149, 154, 155, 158
    Arabic, Christian, 17

inscriptions (cont.)
  Arabic, modern, 51, 136, 138, 139
  Armenian, 8, 18, 20, 21, 26, 40, 43, 45, 50, 89, 105, 106, 109, 116, 121, 122
  Armenian, dates of, 21, 46, 106
  Armenian in Wadi Leja, 36, 89
  Armenian, on Mount Sinai peak, 105–8
  Armenian on Saint Catherine's Monastery doors, 116
  Christian, 47, 49
  conditions of writing, 71
  Coptic, 111
  Egyptian hieroglyphs, 40, 41, 154
    destruction of, 41
  English, 45, 79
  Ethiopic, 20
  Georgian, 21, 22, 26, 89, 108, 110, 122, 143, 150
  Georgian, dates of, 94
  Greek, 17, 22, 41, 42, 49, 55, 59, 63, 82, 83, 89–91, 102, 105, 106, 108, 109, 111, 132, 134, 135, 143, 148, 150, 154, 158, 159
  Latin, 40, 44, 45, 154, 161
  locations of, 42–44, 46, 54, 55, 62, 71, 83, 93, 112, 122, 126, 127, 131, 134
  Nabatean, 17, 18, 22, 29, 37, 41, 42, 47, 48–51, 55, 56, 58, 59, 63, 71, 74, 75, 78, 79, 82, 89, 112, 139, 140, 143, 148, 150, 154
  Nabatean, ancient, 22, 43
  Nabatean, purpose of, 50, 112
  Old North Arabic, 40, 154, 155
  publication of, 93
  Russian, 40, 51
  South Arabic, 78
  strange, 158
  Thamudic, 111
insects, spider, 141
Isaiah, book of 41:19, 81
Israel, *passim*
  Academy of Sciences, 9
  Museum, 143
  Sinai Administration, 34

Israel-Egypt peace. *See* Egypt-Israel peace agreement
Israeli Military Government, 2, 9, 16, 32
Israelites, 22, 37, 49
Jebel Adir, 102
Jebel Ashka, 55
Jebel Baraqa, 22, 23, 43, 137, 138
Jebel Ḥemiyar, 74
Jebel Katerina. *See* Mount Catherine
Jebel Moneijat, 102
Jebel Moneijat Musa, 46, 51
  description of, 51
  sacred to bedouin, 51
Jebel Musa. *See* Mount Sinai
Jebel Safsafa, 48, 89, 102, 108, 110
  survey of, 103
Jebel Serbal, 37, 51, 68
Jerusalem, 1, 6–8, 11, 28, 69, 148, 151, 153, 154
Jezirat Farun, 12
Jordan, Kingdom of, 17, 124
Judean Desert, 81
Justinian, Emperor, 32, 100
Kraemer, Casper J., Jr., 74
Lake, Kirsopp, 59
Lewis, Agnes Smith, 101
limestone, 140
logistics, 9, 11, 35, 36, 58, 61, 86
MacDonald, Major C. K., 42
malaria, 83
Mamluk, 12
manuscripts,
  Caucasian Albanian, 116
  Christian Arabic, 116
  discovery of, 116
  Georgian, 116
  Greek, 116
  Syriac, 116
Mayerson, Philip, 12, 27, 74, 94, 145
Melitene, 6
Mesrop, Saint, 18
mining, 80, 81, 142, 158. *See also* geology
Mitzpeh Ramon, 155, 156
Moise, Yael, 2
monasticism, in Sinai, 33, 34, 112

INDEX

monks
  ascetic, 33
  work of, 112
mosaic, Bird, 8
mosaic, Eustathius, 8
mosaics, at Saint Catherine's Monastery, 32
Moses, 7, 21, 33
Moses's rock, 49, 90, 145
  description of, 90
  new chapel near, 91
mosque, inside Saint Catherine's Monastery, 100
mosquitos, 157
Mount Catherine, 14, 32, 48, 61, 70, 105
Mount Horeb, 48, 102, 145
Mount Karkom, 156
Mount Sinai, *passim*
  airfield, 69
  ascent of, 102
  descriptions of, 102–5, 112
  grotto, 106
  peak, 7, 105
  peak, buildings on, 105
  stairs, 104, 108, 109
  tourists at, 113
Nabatean sanctuaries and temples, 37, 46, 51, 68, 69, 126
Nabatean titles, 51
Nabatean-Byzantine town, 37
Nabateans, 17, 156
  history of, 18
  traders, 58, 156
Naḥal Ovdat, 155
Naqb Budra, 84
Naqb el-Hawa, 39, 47, 61, 62, 63, 89
Naqb Rakna, 68, 70, 73, 75, 78, 122
  description of, 75
  description of descent from, 74
Nature Protection Society, 95
Nature Reserves Authority, 19, 34, 35, 41, 45, 48, 124
Nau, François, 7
Naveh, Joseph, 22, 78
nawamis, 22, 23, 125, 140, 145

Negev Desert, 17, 27, 68, 81, 122, 154, 155, 157, 158
Negev, Abraham, 5, 8, 19, 21, 22, 26, 51, 58–60
Neot HaKikar tours, 22, 114
Nessana, 68, 74, 145
Nessana papyri, 74
Nickel, Douglas R., 59
night sky, 43, 77, 147, 157
Numbers, book of, 11:35, 16
nunnery, 35
Nweiba, 9, 13, 14, 26, 30, 40, 69, 131, 147
Odessa, 115
Ofira, 12
Omariyah, bedouin tribal leader, 72
Ovdat, 154, 155, 156. *See also* 'Ein Ovdat
Ovdat (Obode), 145
Palmer, Edward H., 62–64, 101, 155
papyri,
  Arabic, 74
  Greek, 74
patina, 54, 74, 78, 131, 132, 155–57
Persian Empire, 17
Petra, city, 17, 156
Petrie, W. M. Flinders, 84, 132, 137
petroglyphs. *See* rock drawings
Philadelphia, Pennsylvania, 27, 93
photography, 9, 17
  of the Sinai, history of, 59
  problems of, 23, 24, 27, 28, 58, 60, 61, 105, 123
Piacenza Pilgrim, 145
pilgrim reports, character of, 64
pilgrim travel, 127–28,
pilgrimage, pilgrims, 6, 121
  Armenian, 6, 7
  Christian, 6, 79
  Muslim, routes of, 134
  routes of, 26, 28, 29, 62, 74
  Russian, 40
plant, Burning Bush *rubus sanctu*s, 33, 114
plants, 63, 104
  Arabian rush (Juncus Arabicus), 72
  Belladonna, 63

plants (cont.)
  bladder senna (*Colutea istria*), 156
  Verbascum sinaiticum, 109
  wormwood (*Artemis judaica*), 142
Prescott, H. F. M., 62, 74, 130
Princeton University, 114
Puech, Emile, 20
Radovan, Zev, 123, 124, 131, 133, 151
ramle (sands), 53
Ramleh, city, 73
Ramon Crater, 155
Ras el-Kalb, 138
Ras Zalaqa, 122, 144, 152
Red Sea, 11
reptiles, Sinai agama (*Pseudo-trapelus sinaiticus*), 77
road, ancient and deliberate, 90, 135, 136
roads, 12, 14, 131
  difficulties of, 22, 55, 56, 79, 80
rock drawings, 22, 26, 41, 57–59, 74, 78, 82, 122, 125, 127, 131, 138 140, 143, 148–50, 157, 159
  camels, 18, 155
  dating of, 143
  dogs, 18, 157
  Egyptian, 159
  Egyptian boat, 82
  equestrian saint, 82
  humans, 155, 157
  ibex, 18, 155, 157
  Nabatean, 18
  ostrich hunt, 26
Rock Inscriptions, 153
Rock Inscriptions and Graffiti Project and database, 18, 29, 37, 44, 75, 78, 81, 83, 153, 159
Romania, 30
route, coastal, 132
routes, 39, 52, 53, 62, 67, 70, 79, 93, 102, 103, 121, 122, 129, 134, 144, 151, 156
  ancient, 67, 141
  consideration of, 50, 65
  eastern Sinai, 121, 122, 151
  Tih, 68, 74, 79,
  western Sinai, 67, 68, 122, 121, 122

Saint Catherine, relics of, 114
Saint Catherine's Monastery, 29, 32, 33, 39, 50, 62, 91, 122
  bells, 115
  conditions at, 99, 110
  description of, 91, 92, 114–15, 117
  hostel, 100
  people at, 47, 48
  water and plumbing, 115
Saint Catherine's region, 20, 27, 30, 31, 34, 39, 43, 45, 47, 53, 54, 65, 68, 69, 79, 86, 87, 95
Samuelian, Thomas J. (Tom), 8, 9, 30, 45, 50–52, 57, 69, 92
  indisposition of, 60, 61, 64, 65
sand, rippled, 77
sandstone, 22–54, 57, 59, 140, 155
Saracens, 74
Sass, Benny, 9, 38, 45
Satala, 6
Serabit el-Khadem, 42, 59, 74, 84
Shaked, Abraham, 95
Sharm el-Sheikh, 12
Sharon, Moshe, 21
Shauly, 69, 142, 143
Shefer, Michal, 96–100, 102–5, 108, 112–18
Sheikh 'Atiyah, 137
Sheikh 'Awad, oasis, 47, 63, 89
Sheikh Ghanem, 72
Sheikh Ḥmed, 73
Sheikh Suleyman Nafa'i, 79
sheikhs (tombs of tribal leaders), 72
Sinai, 156
  desert, 2, 11
  eastern, survey of, 31
  rainfall, 137
Sinai Peninsula, 27, 46
"Sinai time", 35
Sophronius, Father, 99, 114, 115
Spain, 33
Stanley, A.P., 16, 17, 29, 37
stone structures, 75, 76, 86, 135, 137, 140, 142
  function of, 76

INDEX

Stone, Aurit, 124, 131, 133
Stone, Dan J., 155
Stone, M.E., 8, 18, 44, 94, 121, 153
stones, structures, 146, 147
Suez, Gulf of, 29, 39, 79
Suleyman ibn Abed al-Malik, Caliph, 73
Tekor, Inscription of, 19
Tel-Aviv, 11
Theodosius, pilgrim, 145
Thresinger, Wilfred, 36, 77, 88
Tih
    escarpment, 65, 68, 70, 73, 75, 78, 145
    passes down from, 65,
    visible from Mount Sinai, 105
Tilford, Nicole, 2
Timna, 158, 159,
Tiridates III, King, 1
Tischendorf, C. von, 115
travel, conditions of, 43
trees,
    acacia, 80, 135, 137
    Atlantic pistachio, 156
tribal patterns, 58
turquoise, 41, 85, 86
    mines, 42, 74, 84
    bedouin sell, 41, 42
    purchase of, 85
tires, repairs of in the field, 87
Ulm, 6
Umm 'Araq, 77, 78, 79
University of Michigan, 114
University of Pennsylvania, 9, 27, 67, 93, 96
Uvda,
    airport, 133
    valley, 158,
Venice, 6
Wadi Abu Ghad'ayat, 148
Wadi Abu Natash, 53, 65, 68, 76–81
    mining destroyed inscriptions, 82
Wadi Abu Tarifiyeh, 142
Wadi Aḥdar, 69, 70
Wadi 'Ajar, 72
Wadi Arade, 26, 32,, 55–57
Wadi Ashka, 56

Wadi Ber(r)a, 47
Wadi Bireq, 72, 73
Wadi Budra, 79, 80, 84
Wadi Buwera, 47
Wadi el-'Ein, 14
Wadi El-Arba'in. *See* Wadi Leja
Wadi el-Deir, 50, 51, 100, 110
Wadi el-Ḥesi, 122, 135, 137, 138, 141, 143–46
Wadi el-Sheikh, 37, 47, 67
Wadi Feiran, identified with Rephidim, 37
Wadi Feiran, oasis, 37, 39, 46, 51, 53, 67–69, 86, 87, 122
Wadi Ghalem, 140
Wadi Ghazale, 126, 127, 129, 146–48
Wadi Ḥajjaj (Ḥaggag), 5, 8, 26, 31, 40, 45, 52, 54, 55, 57, 70, 83, 124, 144, 146–49
    description of, 16
    Rock I, 22, 59
    Rock II, 21, 59, 60
    Rock III, 17, 19–22, 25, 31, 59, 61, 123
    Rock III, inscriptions on, 20, 60
    Rock IV, 22, 59
    Rock V, 21, 22, 25
    Rock VI, 21
    Rock VIII, 17,18, 22, 150
    Rock X, 58, 59
    Rock XI, 149
    Rock XII, 149
    Rock XIII 150
    rocks in, 16
    survey of, 31, 59, 61, 118, 121
Wadi Ḥudra, 126, 149
Wadi Iqna, 41
Wadi Leja, 29, 35, 36, 47, 48, 51, 52, 54, 70, 89, 100, 102, 103, 110, 112, 115
    description of, 49, 111, 112
    gardens in, 36, 112
    paved path in, 89, 110
Wadi Maghara, 9, 38–42, 67, 69, 84, 85, 137
Wadi Mara, 55, 126, 131
Wadi Mukattab, 22, 29, 37, 38, 39, 42, 45, 52, 54, 65, 67, 68, 79, 83, 86, 117, 122

Wadi Nisrin, 46
Wadi Rum, 56, 57, 125, 126
   description of, 126
   sand "dune" in, 56, 57, 126
Wadi Sa'ad, 138, 145
Wadi Sa'al, 61, 131, 147
Wadi Shellaleh, 45, 80–83
   description of, 82
Wadi Sidri, 3, 79, 86
   Upper, 134, 144
   Upper, description of 134, 135
Wadi Siḥ, 72–74, 76, 78, 79
   description of mouth of, 76, 77
   rocky outcropping in, 77
Wadi Sulaf, 47, 61, 63,
Wadi Sweir, 131
Wadi Tlaḥ, 65, 70,
   description of, 64,
Wadi Watir, 122, 126, 130, 146,147,
Wadi Zalaqa, 118, 119, 121, 141, 142, 144–46
Wadi Zarniyeh, 140
wadis, 5
   floods in, 32
   function of, 31, 32
   travel in, 31, 32, 63

Wallachia, 30
Wasdi HaJ Rock XIII, 150
wasem (bedouin tribal mark), 138
wasems, 138, 155, 157,
Wasserstein, Abraham, 45
water, 12, 61, 85, 85, 108
   no camping by, 83, 84, 131, 132
   no pollution of, 49
Waṭiyeh Pass, 37, 55
Weitzmann, Kurt, 114
Well of Miriam, 115
White Canyon, 127, 148
Whitney, William K., 108
Wilkinson, John, 145
writing, 6
   Arabic, 17, 18, 41
   Armenian, majuscule and minuscule, 45
   Coptic, 111
   Nabatean, 22, 41, 56
   Nabatean, development of 17, 18
   Old North Arabic, 41
   Safaitic, 58

www.ingramcontent.com/pod-product-compliance
Lightning Source LLC
Chambersburg PA
CBHW021709230426
43668CB00008B/780